THE *art* OF TRADING

A Complete Guide to Trading
The Australian Markets

2nd Edition

Christopher Tate

Wrightbooks

First edition first published by Wrightbooks in November 1997, reprinted August 1998 and June 1999.

This edition published 2001 by Wrightbooks
an imprint of John Wiley & Sons Australia, Ltd
42 McDougall Street, Milton Qld 4064

Office also in Melbourne

Typeset in 12/13.2 AGaramond

© Christopher Tate 2001

Reprinted November 2001, March 2004, August 2007, September 2009 and March 2012

National Library of Australia Cataloguing-in-publication data:

Tate, Christopher.
The art of trading: a complete guide to trading the Australian markets.

2nd ed.
Includes index.
ISBN 1 876627 63 8

1. Stocks – Australia. 2. Portfolio management.
3. Investment analysis. I. Title.

332.63220994

Cover design by Rob Cowpe

10 9 8 7 6

Disclaimer

The material in this book is of the nature of general comment only, and neither purports nor intends to be advice. Readers should not act on the basis of any matter in this book without considering (and, if appropriate, taking) professional advice with due regard to their own particular circumstances. The author and publisher expressly disclaim all and any liability to any person, whether a purchaser of this publication or not, in respect of anything and of the consequences of anything done or omitted to be done by any such person in reliance, whether whole or partial, upon the whole or any part of the contents of this publication.

CONTENTS

(Cont'd)

CONTENTS (CONT'D)

PREFACE

IF YOU ARE READING THIS BOOK in the belief that it will make you rich, forget it. I have no magic secret. I don't have a super secret indicator that will allow you to trade with impunity. I have partially discovered what I believe to be the pivotal concept in trading, but it took me many years and I did not find it where I expected to when I initially began this odyssey.

I make mistakes trading. It is quite a regular occurrence for me to look at the market and simply shake my head and wonder why price moved in a particular way. Even more regular is me simply asking: why on earth did I do that? But then trading is nothing if not interesting.

Trading is not what most people imagine it to be. Forget the hype merchants, liars and charlatans who have crawled out from under some slimy rock in the past few years. There is no system that will allow you to get 90% of all trades right. There is no magic options strategy that is risk-free and simply allows you to count your ever-expanding bank balance. Trading is hard. It is not a skill that can be mastered simply by buying a magic piece of software. If it were that easy don't you think that the giant hedge funds and Commodity Trading Advisers who regularly make returns in excess of 50% per annum would simply shut down their trading operations and buy a piece of software? There would be no need for them to analyse markets, look at crowd behaviour or constantly search for innovative ways to control risk. They could simply buy a piece of software.

It should be remembered that most traders fail and fail dismally. As you embark on your trading career you will no doubt encounter a defining moment. This moment will generally revolve around a catastrophic loss and your response to it. You have not lived as a trader or as a human being unless you have stood and looked at the wreckage of your endeavours. Everyone who is still fascinated by markets even after decades of exposure has had such an epiphany. It is in this moment that you will decide whether you really want to master trading to the degree necessary to be profitable and to enjoy your time in the markets. You should be cautioned—you will never master the market, you will merely be fortunate enough to go in the direction it is going. And in time you may generate enough wisdom to realise when it is going in a direction that you are uncomfortable with and what the appropriate response should be.

In writing this book I have tried to distil some of the many errors I have made and the reasons for those errors. I have a personal aversion to people writing about how good they are. You don't learn anything from such enterprises.

Christopher Tate
Melbourne
March 2001

Part I

PSYCHOLOGY

"I can calculate the motions of the heavenly bodies
but not the madness of people."

Sir Isaac Newton, 1720

1   THE PSYCHOLOGY
OF TRADING

AT THE START OF THIS SECTION on the psychology of trading I need to make a blunt point; only an amateur believes that trading is about indicators, company reports, shareholder meetings and broker recommendations. Trading is a psychological endeavour. Markets are little more than herds of humans, each with competing beliefs and underlying biases. As such, markets are loaded with emotional energy, all of it irrational in nature. It is easy for traders to become infected with this irrationality and behave in exactly the same manner as the crowd. You may argue with this if you wish but in doing so you will merely betray your status as a novice. Even Sir Isaac Newton, whose quote opens this book, fell victim to this irrationality when he was caught in the collapse of the South Sea Bubble.

I do not follow the crowd, so I have written this book in the reverse order to what you might traditionally expect—the section on indicators has been placed at the end. Before moving onto the psychology of trading I will ask you to think about the graphic below and see if you can work out what it represents. I have placed the answer at the end of this chapter.

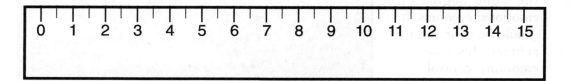

THE EMOTIONAL JOURNEY

Shown below is a roller-coaster, which reflects the emotional journey of the amateur trader; each win is greeted with exaltation and each loss with absolute despair. Such swings are indicative of a complete lack of control over the emotions that come from trading.

THE AMATEUR TRADER'S EMOTIONAL JOURNEY

It is impossible for a trader to control the market. The only arena of control traders have is self-control; without self-control the trader is lost. Markets are ruthless; they do not care if people cannot control themselves. As a colleague of mine once stated, when the market runs people over it not only reverses over them a few times, it gets out, tap dances on their heads and then drives off, only to return and repeat the process all over again just in case they didn't get the message to get out of the way the first time.

THE PROFESSIONAL TRADER'S EMOTIONAL JOURNEY

Professional traders display emotions that are more in line with this image; calm and relaxed, without any enormous peaks or troughs. Each win or loss is greeted with the same degree of emotional evenness. It should be your aim to achieve this state of emotional control.

4

THE LEARNED BEHAVIOUR OF TRADERS

There are, I believe, ten significant blunders that all poor traders are prone to make, and—in no particular order of importance—they are as follows.

Tate's Ten Significant Blunders

1. Undercapitalisation

Most traders come to the market with grandiose dreams of what can be done. I have had people approach me in seminars convinced that they can make $1,500 per day from a $10,000 trading float.

Many accounts are undercapitalised from the start, and as such they suffer from an inability to withstand many drawdowns before they collapse. This is particularly true in derivatives markets. The available evidence suggests that in futures markets an account under $50,000 has little hope of survival, yet traders are repeatedly drawn to the Share Price Index contract with under $10,000 in their accounts.

> **"You must have a comprehensive plan for engaging the market. No plan, no profit—it is that simple."**

One of the joys of trading is that you are your own boss (although for many this is hard to take), and therefore you are the quintessential small business. But many small businesses fail from being undercapitalised—trading is no different.

2. Reliance on external sources

If brokers, financial planners or fund managers knew what they were doing they would be doing it, not talking to you. The failure rate in trading is high—in futures markets the rate of failure is as high as nine out of ten—so simple statistics dictate that your chances of finding someone who knows more than you are remote. Listen to others at your own peril.

3. Lack of a trading plan

When it comes to trading there are no rules. The stock exchange does not impose rules on how you should trade (apart from the normal rules of business conduct), nor will the market teach you how to trade. You must have a comprehensive plan for engaging the market. No plan, no profit—it is that simple.

4. Inconsistent application of a trading plan

Some traders have a plan of sorts but it is little more than a collection of random meanderings that are applied on an inconsistent basis.

5. *Not taking losses*

I never met a big loss that was not once a small loss.

6. *Cutting profits too soon*

I never met a big profit that was not once a small profit.

7. *Misunderstanding how markets operate*

Many novice traders enter the market without the slightest knowledge of how it actually works. They do not properly understand how to place an order nor do they have any idea of basic terminology. Novices are also easily swayed by conspiracy theories as an explanation of why they are unable to make money.

8. *Lack of confidence*

Trading is a difficult business. There are moments when things do not go as planned. This is to be expected, but a chronic lack of confidence can lead to pre-emptive moves out of positions or a failure to act when required.

9. *Performance anxiety*

Successful traders accept that they will have losing trades but these are not a reflection of who they are. Everyone makes mistakes.

10. *Fear of the unknown*

Markets present us with a unique challenge. We never know the outcome of a trade until we close it down. We constantly operate in the unknown and this is too much for some people. We are creatures of comfort. The unknown can fill us with trepidation and fear.

The intriguing thing about these ten behaviours is that each one has largely been learned. Traders often look to the market to learn how to trade, but it has often been said that the market will teach you how *not* to trade simply because it will draw out and reinforce all those areas of your personality that guarantee failure.

It is necessary to understand how traders have learned to do the wrong thing at the wrong time so that we can then see how to rectify these errors. The flow chart opposite is a schematic of how a poor trader makes a trading decision. You will notice that the key to this entire chain of events is the identification of a signal and an inappropriate initial response to that signal.

FIGURE 1.1   THE DECISION-MAKING TREE OF A POOR TRADER

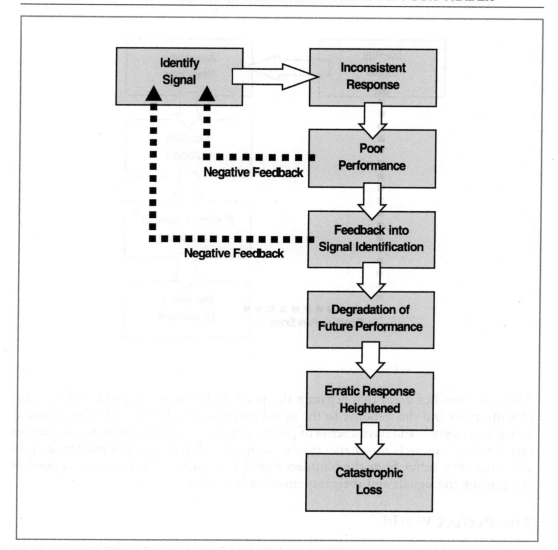

Now compare this with the decision-making tree of a good trader (overleaf). The differences between the way good and poor traders make decisions were identified by Jake Bernstein, author of *The Investors Quotient*. Notice how this tree is arranged around the positive reinforcement of all aspects of the trading process. Each time a trade is successfully completed the natural tendency is for this successful behaviour to be reinforced.

FIGURE 1.2 THE DECISION-MAKING TREE OF A GOOD TRADER

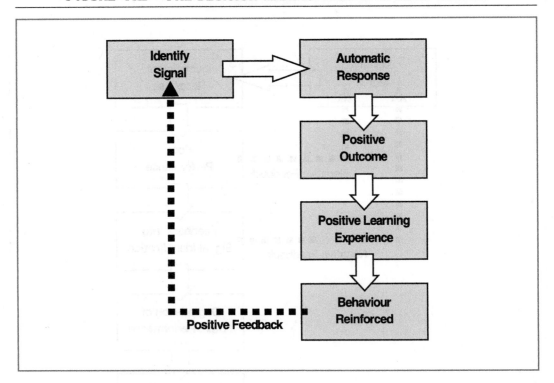

There are two key areas that separate the poor trader from the good trader; signal identification and the response to the signal that is received. Top traders are better at recognising signals and have a series of pre-programmed responses that do not vary. In essence their trading is automatic; they see a signal and they act. Poor traders don't do this since they suffer from the blunders highlighted earlier. They are not as good at recognising the signals and their responses are inconsistent.

The Perfect World

To understand how this dichotomy between the good and poor trader has occurred it is necessary to have a look at the way traders have built up their battery of responses. To do this we need to break the world up into the real world and the perfect world.

In the perfect world a trader learns to trade in the following way:

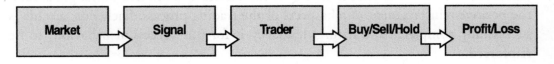

The market presents the trader with a signal, the trader then acts upon this signal by either buying, selling or holding a given instrument and this action results in a profit or loss. This chain is very similar to the trading process of the successful trader. This is to be expected since the responses of top traders have been optimised by experience. It would be impossible to find a top trader who did not have an approach to trading that was similar to this perfect-world view.

As an example, let's assume we have a trader using a simple moving average crossover system with appropriate money management. If this system were profitable then in a perfect world the trader would only act upon the signals generated by the trading system. As such the trader would become more and more profitable. But this is not what happens. In the real world successful traders become more and more successful whilst poor traders remain poor traders until they eventually self-destruct.

The perfect-world view encounters difficulty in the area of signal identification. The trader must have a trigger for taking any action. This trigger must reflect the individual's own system or way of doing things. However, it is possible to receive a signal to act but then to encounter a conflicting signal; this conflicting signal can come from something that the trader has read or been told. It is a natural tendency for humans to abrogate responsibility to what is perceived as a higher authority. The question I am most-often asked is, "What is your view about ABC?" This is a question that is asked countless times every day in chat forums around the world. It is a plaintive cry for reinforcement and justification for taking any given action. It also betrays a trader's status as an amateur. It is a question to which I never respond since I know that it interrupts the trader's natural decision-making process. It also does not matter what others think, just as it does not matter what I think. We may all be wrong and you may be right.

This signal conflict has two possible outcomes. Firstly the external source can be ignored and the trader acts on the original signal. This is the best outcome. If the original signal turned out to be correct then a positive learning experience takes place and the successful behaviour is reinforced. Even if the signal does not give a profitable result this is a positive experience because the trading system used is being tested under real-world conditions.

The second possible outcome is that the conflicting signal is taken. If a loss is then incurred then this is not a bad result; this is actually a good result since the system being employed is being tested under real-world conditions. From a trading point of view it also a good result because a loss is being taken without hesitation, displaying a skill that is the preserve of the professional trader.

If the conflicting signal is taken and the trader makes a profit, this is actually the worst possible result. The bad behaviour (i.e. accepting the outside advice) is reinforced and is therefore more likely to be repeated in the future.

The responses of traders can be summarised by the following table:

Signal	Response	Outcome	Evaluation
System	Follow	Loss	Positive
System	Follow	Profit	Positive
External	Nil	Nil	Positive
External	Follow	Loss	Positive
External	Follow	Profit	Negative

The only experiences that matter are those that arise from your own trading system. Losing traders have learned to be losing traders and winning traders have learned to be winning traders. This process of learning to be a winning trader has come from the traders being self-reliant and only taking notice of their own signals.

INTUITIVE TRADING

If I were to pose the question, "What is the next number in this series: 1, 2, 3, 4, 5, 6, ... ?" the overwhelming majority of individuals would know. Likewise if I asked, "What are the next letters in this series: m, n, o, p, q, ... ?" the vast majority would be able to answer correctly. In fact the answer would come so quickly to most that no conscious thought would seem to precede the answer. The answer has been arrived at intuitively; there is no need for conscious thought since the answer is already known and stored deep within the subconscious. Trading should elicit the same speed in the execution of trading decisions.

Successful trading relies upon the development, cultivation and conditioning of habits that influence the way the market is seen. Successful trading does not revolve around the acquisition of new indicators. Trading is in its purest form an intuitive endeavour where decisions are made instantly.

Trading on the Right Side of the Brain

To understand how trading decisions can be made easier it is necessary to understand how the brain processes information. It is common knowledge that the brain is split into two halves. The left side has a need to habituate existing behaviour and to see the world through a very logical rational framework. The left side of the brain is the primary information processing area. In contrast, the right side of the brain acts as a clearing house for intuitive and creative functions. The right side is capable of intuitive leaps that often transcend the available information. The right side of the brain can be a valuable ally to the trader if it is trained correctly.

To better understand the dichotomy between the right and left side consider the following contrast in functionality.

Left Brain	Right Brain
Analytical	Imaginative
Objective	Subjective
Deductive	Inductive
Time bound	Timeless
Scientific	Artistic
Logical	Unconscious
Rational	Intuitive
Intellectual	Emotional

Traders face a problem: all information received by the right side is re-routed to the left side for processing and comment. The reason for this is that the left side is so important to normal routine functioning that it has overshadowed the right side. Unfortunately for the trader the right side of the brain is the key to flexibility; it is the key to changing existing thought-patterns.

You will only succeed as a trader if you change the way you think. The challenge for traders is not to accumulate new methods of analysis or more indicators, it is to challenge existing thought-patterns and habits.

Ken No San

The closest parallel that can be found to the intuitive state of trading is the state of 'Ken No San', or 'no-mindedness'. This is a state achieved by samurai warriors before combat. The samurai had a strong motivation to remove the conscious mind from their activities. Decisions had to be made by samurai warriors in fractions of a second—the slightest hesitation could result in their heads leaving their shoulders. As such the conscious mind was an impediment to survival, so strategies had to be generated that removed conscious thought from the heat of combat. The aim was to have behaviours that were automatic.

Your trading needs to reach this state of discipline—when a signal is seen it must be taken without hesitation. I am not suggesting that you go out and subject yourself to the rigorous lifestyle of a medieval samurai, but I am suggesting that you compare and contrast the intuitive trading styles with those that are subjective and based on conscious decisions. The following table will give you an indication of the differences.

Intuitive Trading Process	Subjective Trading Process
Creates optimism	Creates anxiety, fear and anger
Is challenging and fun	Makes traders psychologically ill-prepared
Provides calm mental state	Results in low level of performance
Results in high level of performance	

> *"Your trading needs to reach this state of discipline—when a signal is seen it must be taken without hesitation."*

The difference between the two styles of trading is immediately apparent. Traders who are intuitive in the way they view the market are optimistic about the opportunities that the market offers. To them trading is fun. This removes much of the fear that can be associated with the market. It is this fear that generates the anxiety felt by the subjective trader. The intuitive trader is calm in the belief that the market will go in the direction it decides to go in. Subjective traders have trouble accepting that their skills will guide them through the market. They also struggle with their lack of control over the market. Intuitive traders have a high level of performance in part because of their acceptance of all possible outcomes. Subjective traders become consumed by their inability to control the market, and as such they perform very poorly.

12

There are three basic rules to assist you in engaging your intuition in trading:

1.   Do not try to pick the high; and

2.   Do not try to pick the low. These are beyond your control.

3.   And finally, let the market—and not your ego—dictate the direction of your trade.

Factors Leading to an Intuitive State of Mind

Mental Relaxation

Traders must be calm and display a high degree of concentration. A state of inner turmoil leads to mistakes. Do not trade when you are distressed for any reason. Should you attempt to trade whilst distressed then the market will appear to be moving too fast, decision-making becomes difficult and a negative feedback loop is initiated. (See Chapter 3 for more on relaxation.)

Physical Calmness

A physically calm state leads to mental tranquillity. Tension and relaxation are mutually exclusive—should you be physically on edge this will translate to your mental state.

It is possible for traders to monitor the way they feel on an ongoing basis. Take time out during the trading day to do a systems check.

Confidence

If you are not confident in your ability to engage the market then do not enter it. Take some more time and continue with your preparation.

Top traders have positive expectations as to what trading will bring them—they are confident of their long-term success. Many novice traders increase their lack of confidence with the images they process. Many novices regard trading as a form of conflict such as war. War is a very powerful image and carries with it numerous associated emotions, none of which are positive. These associated emotions can reduce the confidence of a trader. The images that are processed by your conscious mind are under your control, so don't fall into this trap.

Optimism

All good traders possess an optimistic demeanour. They believe that they can succeed in any market anywhere in the world at any time. This is different from arrogance, it is merely being self-assured. Much of this comes from the way they view various outcomes. Consider the differences in the way a good trader and a poor trader view the two possible outcomes of a trade (shown overleaf).

13

	Winning Trades	Losing Trades
Good Trader	Permanent	Temporary
	Pervasive	Rare
	Personal	Impersonal
Poor Trader	Temporary	Permanent
	Rare	Pervasive
	Impersonal	Personal

Notice how the matrix for the good trader is the exact opposite to that of the poor trader.

Focus

I have found that focus is the key towards developing intuition, and it is also the key to discipline. It may border on cliche but the past is gone, the future is yet to happen. Bad trades fade into the past and the future may offer a limitless number of potentially good trades but the only point in time that matters is what is happening now. Too many traders live in the past. This is particularly the preserve of the hobby chartist (as opposed to the trader who uses charts). The hobbyist is continually looking back and saying, "If only I had taken such and such a trade when such and such an indicator said to." The harsh truth is that this particular trade is gone forever and it will never return.

You can learn to focus by having a methodical approach to the market. Each part of an analysis builds upon the last thereby bringing you to a point where a decision can be made.

If you have lost focus there are some simple tricks that can restore it. Firstly leave the market immediately. Markets cannot be traded in a half-hearted way. From there consider your trading goals and why the achievement of these goals is important to you. What must you do to achieve these goals and how do you prepare mentally and physically for the attainment of these goals? You are asking yourself what price must be paid for the achievement of these goals. This is a constant self-diagnostic technique which will tell you instantly whether you are sufficiently focused to continue trading. If you cannot readily answer the questions that relate to the attainment of your goals then withdraw from the market until you can.

The Answer

I promised at the beginning of this chapter to give you the answer as to what the ruler represented. It is simple: it is the difference between you and a highly successful trader. The distance separating you from a highly successful trader is under 15 centimetres. This is the distance from ear to ear of the average person.

Trading is conducted in the mind and nowhere else. You can disbelieve this if you choose, but you will fail— I guarantee it.

> *"The distance separating you from a highly successful trader is under 15 centimetres. This is the distance from ear to ear of the average person."*

2 CREATING THE MINDSET OF A PROFITABLE TRADER

In CHAPTER 1 WE LOOKED AT the psychological aspects of trading and the characteristics of good and poor traders. We also looked at ways to improve your approach to the markets. In this chapter we will look at ways to further improve the way you view markets.

I will begin this chapter by asking a question:

Is failure likely for traders?

The answer to this is unfortunately *yes*, the majority of people who attempt to trade will fail and fail dismally. They will fail not because they lack a powerful enough computer or they don't have cable TV or their broker is an idiot or because the new sine-wave-corrected low-fat twin-overhead-cam moving average doesn't work properly. They will fail because of the people they are.

Traders have been failing in droves ever since there have been markets. Markets have seduced the best and the brightest—none are immune. Even Sir Isaac Newton—probably one of the five smartest humans to have ever lived—was caught by the speculative fervour surrounding the South Sea Bubble.

Don't be too depressed by this—to a degree it is not your fault. You have been hard-wired to fail. I am not talking about such babble as your mother didn't hug you enough or you were dropped on your head when young. I am referring to the way evolution

17

has hard-wired the brain to respond in a certain way under certain circumstances. It is this hard-wiring that prompts most traders to engage in behaviour that guarantees their failure.

The types of behaviour that guarantee failure can be examined in the context of traders' responses to various situations they might find themselves in. To understand fully these responses we need to go back to the days of the caveman.

THE DEVELOPMENT OF HUMAN PSYCHOLOGY

Life for your average caveman must have been inordinately harsh. Each day survival was at the forefront of all activities. As such it was paramount to avoid any form of loss—when you are living a desperate hand-to-mouth existence then to lose a little may mean you lose your life.

It may seem that this sort of background would naturally predispose us to be averse to loss. If you consider this in a wider context this would naturally predispose early man to not being a big risk-taker. If you had just enough to get by why take unnecessary risks that may spell disaster for not only you but also your extended family or tribe? If you came across an unexpected bounty such as a tree with fruit or an abandoned carcass the natural response would be to grab whatever could be carried and then run for shelter.

Running Profits

Now consider the old phrase, "You will never go broke taking a profit." This phrase has its roots in the actions of our early ancestors. They were risk-averse for most of their existence. If they saw a profit—an unexpected bounty—they would grab what they could and run. This is precisely the behaviour of most traders; if they have a small profit they are inclined to grab it and run. While one of the most time-honoured maxims in trading is to let your profits run, most traders are completely incapable of doing so. When they make a small gain hundreds of thousands of years of evolution come into play, forcing them to take tiny profits and exit the market. However in doing this they have guaranteed their own destruction. As we will examine in the money management section being able to let your profits run is one of the most fundamental aspects of trading.

> *"...being able to let your profits run is one of the most fundamental aspects of trading."*

Cutting Losses

Just as evolution has made it hard to let profits run it has also made it difficult to cut losses. Imagine that you are a loss-averse caveman. Each day you struggle to survive, hoarding whatever food comes your way through good luck or good management. Some time through the course of your life you would experience a threat by a predator, a natural disaster or a competing tribe. It is safe to assume that in these moments of great stress you would become risk-seeking, doing anything to save yourself from disaster.

This is precisely what the cavemen as traders do—they become risk-seeking when they should be risk-averse. Traditionally, as a stock a novice is holding drops away from the price it was purchased at the novice uses as consolation the thought that the stock is a good stock and that good stocks get better. As such, when faced with a loss the loss is compounded by buying more (i.e. averaging down). Risk is actively being sought out at a time of threat.

Professional traders understand that when a position moves in the wrong direction they should become risk-averse and exit the position. The novice trader—hamstrung by primitive behaviour—becomes risk-seeking and buys more of the stock. Conversely when faced with a bounty in the form of a position moving in their favour the professionals become risk-seeking and engage in pyramiding. They add to their already profitable position by buying more. The novice—exhibiting all the behaviours of our ancestors—exits the position early and feels better about letting the profit escape by repeating the time-honoured losers' mantra of, "I left something on the table for somebody else." This inability to take losses and let profits run has been termed the disposition effect, and it is a well-known phenomenon among behavioural economists.

Confidence Before Realism

Confidence would have been a key survival element in stone-age times. Those who survived undoubtedly believed they would survive—such confidence would have had an emboldening effect on the individual.

Such a factor would not seem at first to be a limiting factor in trading since confidence is a feature of all top traders. However excessive self-confidence leads to an over-estimation of one's ability to perform certain tasks. In tests administered to drivers, most rated themselves as having above-average driving ability, yet simple probability theory says that 50% of all drivers will have below-average driving ability. This over-confidence permeates the trading arena as well.

Terrance Odean, an Associate Professor in behavioural finance at the University of California Graduate School of Management, analysed over 35,000 brokerage accounts. The most striking thing about Odean's work is that he found that active trading significantly lowered returns from a given pool of funds. Active trading is a reflection of over-confidence. Most traders believe that they must be in the market constantly and that their level of skill allows them to engage the market all the time.

An interesting thing about over-confidence is that it is not gender specific but it does have a distinct gender drift. Odean found that males traded 45% more than women. This active trading actually reduced the performance of the males by 2.65% per year, whereas in the females it reduced trading returns by 1.72% per year. Men traditionally rate their level of confidence as being higher than that of women in what are perceived to be more masculine tasks. Men report trading as being a masculine task that they should excel at, hence they display a greater degree of over-confidence than women.

This over-confidence can be seen in an interesting side effect: traders believe that they are somehow capable of influencing the market. This may seem like a ludicrous suggestion but consider this: have you ever watched people filling out lottery tickets by hand? Why do people fill out a ticket by hand (as opposed to having it filled out by a computer) in a game that is determined purely by chance? The answer curiously enough is that they believe that by doing so they influence the outcome of the event. This may sound irrational but the majority of traders *are* irrational.

Gossip

Trading is essentially an information-management exercise. It requires traders to sift through vast reams of data to seek out trading opportunities. The most efficient way to undertake this exercise is to engage objective criteria that simply look for movement in indices or stocks based upon whatever areas are of interest. Unfortunately many traders sabotage their chances of success by having a random set of inputs in their trading system, the most insidious of which is the tip or the rumour.

The Internet

The Internet has brought with it a vast increase in the resources available to the trader. There is now simply no limit to the amount of information that can be downloaded to the desktop PC. But this revolution in communication has brought with it a hidden downside—the ability for people to propagate rumour and misinformation on a grand scale.

The Internet has enabled the spreading of gossip at an extraordinary rate, largely facilitated by the evolution of the chat room or forum. A benign interpretation of these facilities is that they are the twenty-first century equivalent of the town hall social or perhaps a specialised club where ideas and information are exchanged. Much is made of the view that chat rooms are really an extension of the old share club idea.

A more pragmatic view of chat rooms is that they are the equivalent of a gossip magazine where the gullible are led by the ignorant, and that they promote a variation on the group-think so essential for the formation of a crowd or mob. The chat room is a hot house for misinformation and rumour.

Gordon Allport, in *The Psychology of Rumor*, defines 'rumour' as a specific proposition or belief, passed along from person to person usually by word of mouth without secure standards of evidence being present. This is the hallmark of market-based gossip or rumour. There is no rigorous standard of evidence applied to any of the statements made by individuals. This definition can be applied to both 'factual' information (in the form of the passing on of trading techniques and the like) and also information regarding specific instruments. Stock manipulation or ramping is a problem, and the all-too-human weakness of listening to it is an enormous problem. I don't think this is a major issue with forums, although there have been one or two celebrated instances of attempts to manipulate stocks in a forum.

Most ramping is very unsophisticated. I believe the real danger posed by the technology, and our desperate desire to abrogate responsibility to a higher authority and to feel that we are somehow in the loop, is that most people in chat rooms simply do not know what they are talking about. They have all the hallmarks of propagators of mass excitement, where the participants feel that normal expectations and behaviours no longer exist. They also dissolve that critical self-assessment that is so necessary in trading.

A simple strategy for dealing with the insidious impact of gossip is to simply ignore it. Log-off from chat rooms and forums, cancel your membership to share clubs and go about your own business.

Insider Trading

The perception of having inside information is one of the most dangerous traps novices can fall into. About the only time I would agree with Warren Buffett is that with a million dollars and enough inside information you can go broke.

Novices are attracted to what they perceive to be a tip or inside information for evolutionary reasons. Early primate societies undoubtedly had rapidly shifting power structures. Those who survived were those who understood these shifts in power and swiftly adjusted to them. Since there was no evening news to inform individuals of these changes the only way they could be communicated was by very informal mechanisms, one of which evolved into what we call gossip. Humans love to feel as if they are in the loop or that they have the inside running.

Emotion Before Reason

All situations we encounter are filtered by our emotions first. They are then subject to logical interpretation. In the caveman days powerful instincts were valuable for survival —cognitive processing was a luxury that could not be afforded in times of stress. The same condition affects traders who react without analysing a given situation. This type of response often compounds the responses I have talked about earlier, particularly the impact of gossip. Poor traders simply do not take time to analyse the situations they find themselves in.

There is an additional difficulty created by referring to the market in emotive terms. As I have mentioned earlier imagery is very powerful for individual traders and the images that are processed will affect the way they trade. If they have images that are negative then this will influence the way they respond to a given situation. As was mentioned earlier when I spoke about the caveman as a trader much of the wiring in the brain is left over from a time before markets. A lot of it is extremely primitive. This primitive programming is built around the fight or flight responses, both of which are completely inappropriate to the trader. The fight response causes the trader to become risk-seeking in moments of stress, whereas the flight response may cause the trader to pre-emptively exit the market.

CHARACTERISTICS OF TOP TRADERS

If failure is likely because of human psychology then it is necessary to understand what types of features make up the psychological profile of a profitable trader. If I were to quickly generate a list of the characteristics that describe top traders I would get a list that included the following:

- ⇒ Confident
- ⇒ Organised
- ⇒ Disciplined
- ⇒ Self-reliant
- ⇒ Motivated
- ⇒ Self-contained
- ⇒ Determined
- ⇒ Focused
- ⇒ Independent
- ⇒ Proactive
- ⇒ Objective.

All of these characteristics are diametrically opposed to those we have discussed already (see the 'ten blunders' looked at in the first chapter). The success of top traders lies in their mindset. This contrast can best be viewed by examining common trading considerations and seeing how good traders and poor traders respond.

Losing Trades

Poor Traders

Poor traders regard the health of their trading float as reflecting their own self-worth. When their account goes up they feel good, when it goes down they feel betrayed. If their account started at $20,000 and falls to $10,000 they feel as if their sense of self-worth has halved. This is a common feature of markets; everyone is a genius on the way up, everyone is bereft on the way down.

Poor traders regard a bad situation as being permanent—once they have lost, the losses will continue forever. Poor traders have an accessory belief that hinders them further. They believe that they must never lose any money. This doesn't fit with the belief that losses should be culled instantly. To cull a loss you must take it first. If you believe that you can never lose money then it will be impossible to take a loss. This attitude results in the catastrophic losses that novice traders so frequently experience. Large losses are generally small losses that have simply gotten out of hand.

Good Traders

Professional traders believe that losses are part of the business of trading and as such they are inevitable. Their belief structure is centered around the following points:

1. All professionals have a bad day. Good traders accept their losses because the ability to take a loss is indicative of being a professional trader who is in control.

2. The ability to take losses is a sign of the confidence good traders have in their long-term viability.

3. The ability to take losses frees traders from being concerned about such things—they have accepted what the worst-case scenario is. This acceptance enhances the ability to trade and to take opportunities.

Making Money

Poor Traders

For poor traders making money is the sole focus of why they trade. They concentrate purely on how much they perceive they are going to make. They start to picture all the things they are going to buy and the lifestyle they will lead. But reward can be a phantom. It is quite possible to trade markets for years and never make any money. What does exist is risk. Risk rules the trader's life and this should be the prime focus of the trader. For professional traders making money is not that important. It arises as a side-effect of trading well—trade well and the money comes.

Focusing on the money causes traders to become destabilised. They have difficulty taking losses and their level of stress goes up. This is when they are prone to errors of judgment because of their heightened level of anxiety.

Good Traders

If you trade well you will make money. The paradox of this is that trading well involves taking losses and on occasions losing money.

Beliefs

Poor Traders

Poor traders are particularly inclined to a series of beliefs that are either designed to provide excuses as to why a particular trade went badly or to explain why the market is stopping them from ever being successful. These generally include that the market is rigged, that somehow there is a strange conspiracy that always seems to drive prices in the opposite direction to their trades, or it could be a belief that only insiders make money so that unless you know the right people it is impossible to make money in the market. Even so-called professionals, such as fund managers, have similar limiting beliefs. One of their favourite beliefs is that the market is random. This belief is used to explain why they once again charge the members of their funds for the privilege of yet again underperforming the market.

Good Traders

Before I look at how top traders view the market I need to ask a question: what is the function of the sharemarket? If you come from a corporate finance background your answer might revolve around the capital-raising ability of the market, that in providing this function markets allow businesses to expand their operations and invest in new technologies.

For traders this answer is wrong. The market exists for their personal enrichment—it serves no other function. This is a core belief of top traders; they view the market as their own personal play-thing and as such it holds no fear for them. It is hard to be frightened of something that exists for your benefit.

Working Hard

Poor Traders

By now you may have the idea that trading is difficult, and it is. But the novice actually believes it is easy, that it is simply a matter of reading an occasional issue of *Shares* magazine or looking at a variety of Internet chat rooms. Consider this; would you like to earn say $250,000 per year from trading? The answer is probably *yes*. This is quite a large amount of money and is the equivalent of what an established surgeon or barrister might earn per year. I have friends who are established medical practitioners and barristers. They have been honing their crafts for 15 years or more. Many amateurs believe that they will achieve a similar rate of income with a few minutes a night doing some form of cursory analysis.

Good Traders

The professional knows that the secret of success is hard work and common sense. If you are not prepared to work hard you will not make it. The market does not discriminate on the basis of age, education, sex, or religion. What it does discriminate on is the basis of hard work and discipline. If you are lazy and ill-disciplined the market will point these things out to you.

Taking Responsibility

Poor Traders

There is a simple fact of trading that eludes poor traders and this is that everything they do is their responsibility. If they listened to a broker and the advice resulted in a loss then that is their fault. They decided to listen to the broker. The broker did not come around with a gun and tell them what to buy.

Good Traders

There is within all of us a need to abrogate responsibility to what we perceive to be a higher authority. This is often a necessary feature in order for society to function. Individuals subjugate many of their desires to those of the community. Personal responsibility is something that society does weed out of the individual. However, within the trader personal responsibility is a prerequisite; the trader is responsible for

> *"You make the decision how much you are going to lose and how much you are going to win."*

all actions. This is acknowledged by top traders, and if you are to succeed in trading you must acknowledge that everything is your responsibility. If you win that is your doing. If you lose that is your doing as well. The market takes nothing from you nor does the market give you anything. You make the decision how much you are going to lose and how much you are going to win.

Personality

Poor Traders

The market has no personality other than that which you assign to it. The market is not malevolent, it is not irrational nor is it ill-disciplined. Whenever you see the market as these things what you are seeing is a reflection of your own personality. The market shows you the person you are, not the person you think you are. Under moments of stress people revert to type; if you are ill-disciplined or illogical then the stress of engaging the market will bring this to the fore. The difficulty this creates is that there may be a dislocation between who you think you are and who you really are.

Good Traders

Top traders understand that trading is a journey of self-discovery and that the market is showing them who they really are.

Conclusion

If you have bought a magic system based upon getting rich in 15 minutes per night and it's not working then I am afraid you have fallen into the trap of your own laziness. If you believe trading the markets is this easy then I suggest you peruse a copy of *Market Wizards* by Jack Schwager and learn from his interviews with the world's top traders. What you will learn is that trading is difficult and it does require work. It is no easier to become a trader than it is to wake up one morning and decide that you are going to be neurosurgeon. Successful traders have had long apprenticeships and during these apprenticeships they were often spectacularly unsuccessful. Trading takes work. I have noticed over the years that the easiest way to disturb an audience that I am lecturing to is to mention hard work. Many of the audience are crest-fallen when they discover that trading involves effort and often a great deal of disappointment.

3 CHANGING YOUR PSYCHOLOGY

THE PREVIOUS CHAPTERS ON THE psychology of trading have looked at:

➥ How poor traders have learned many of their responses and how these responses are a reflection of their own hard-wiring. In essence poor traders are trapped by their own primitive ways of viewing the world.

➥ How the mindset of a good trader is vastly different to that of a poor trader.

In this chapter I want to look at how novice traders can examine their own motivations and techniques for trading and mould these to match the mindset of a successful trader.

It is possible to overcome the pitfalls that cause problems early in a trading career. New habits and ways of thinking can be generated. But it must be understood that trading is not a hobby—it is a life-long endeavour. The major part of this journey is about self-discovery, it is not about moving averages, brokers or Internet chat rooms.

The place to start is to look at your own personality.

Determine Your Character

The harsh truth is that you may be unsuitable for trading—you may simply not have the character to trade in any way, shape or form. In an ideal world people would be sufficiently self-aware to make this judgment before they engaged the market and suffered the subsequent stress of a multitude of defeats. Unfortunately this is not the case. It falls to the market to point out to novice traders that they simply don't have what it takes. The market does this by holding a mirror up to their psyche and pointing out the type of person they really are.

To be a successful trader requires discipline, courage, dignity, hard work and honesty. The unfortunate thing is that these virtues are generally out of favour and as such they are unfamiliar to most, yet they are prerequisites for successful trading.

To engage the market you will need a character that is sufficiently robust not only to handle the inevitable defeats that occur but also to allow you to stand on your own and follow your own opinion. This is essential because the desire to have a consensus of opinion is a major distraction for the novice trader. The opinions of others simply do not count in trading.

Accept All Possible Outcomes

Acceptance is that fine line between misery and ecstasy. Traders deal in a world of uncertain outcomes; it is possible that a given trade may be that one stratospheric trade that catapults a trader to a completely new level, or it may be the trade that almost bankrupts a trader. The opportunities that are offered to traders are proportional to the risks that are faced. In Chicago they have what is known as the O'Hare straddle; it is a trade that bankrupts traders and leaves them with only enough money for a plane flight out of O'Hare airport to Brazil.

All outcomes are possible in any given trade. To illustrate this consider the following chart of Biota Holdings.

FIGURE 3.1   BIOTA HOLDINGS

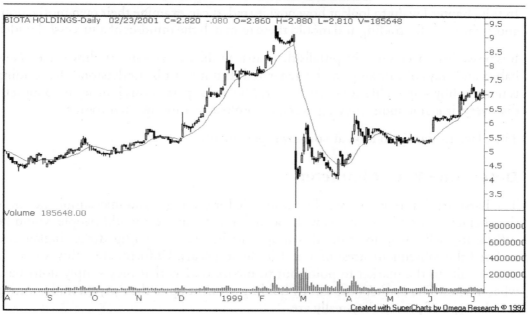

28

The collapse that occurred in February 1999 would not have been picked up by any market surveillance system that I know of. If you are trading then you need to accept that this has the potential to occur at some point during your trading career. There can be no profits without losses just as there can be no rises without falls. If risk cannot be accepted as an essential part of the traders' environment then there is no point attempting to trade. You need to accept this as a reality.

Unfortunately most novices cannot accept this—they believe that there is such a thing as a riskless trade or a trade that is guaranteed. As such it comes as a tremendous disappointment when they fail.

The key to trading success is an optimistic acceptance of all possible outcomes.

Yearn For Success

Success is an intriguing concept—most want it yet few work for it. There seems to be a belief that success is something that just arrives in the mail. You fill in a coupon and bang, it arrives no questions asked. The paradox of success is that most are preprogrammed to avoid it. People will often go out of their way to avoid being successful. Many traders are extraordinarily adept at snatching defeat from the jaws of victory. Legendary trader Jesse Livermore continually went through a boom–bust cycle throughout his trading career. Each time he had reached a level of success an element of his psychology emerged that ensured his destruction.

There is a fear of success within individuals. This fear arises because success brings change and change brings tension and anxiety. These changes may mean moving out of the neighbourhood where you grew up or changing the way you live your life. This can bring an estrangement from friends and family as your life changes. This can be particularly true for the children of migrants where geographical proximity to the family is especially important.

But there is a deeper source of conflict, and that is with established patterns of work. Trading has a work ethic that is very different to established work ethics. A trader has no set routine, no set hours and no recognisable or tangible outcomes for a day's work. This often causes conflict in terms of being perceived to have achieved something during the day. In terms of output to society trading is the most useless activity ever created and from a personal perspective this is something I have struggled with in the past. But then I found a solution after a sabbatical of many years. My solution is that I don't own the money I make, I am merely a conduit. My job is to make it and then give it away. This solved the dilemma for me. Individual traders will need to solve it in their own way.

> *"If risk cannot be accepted as an essential part of the traders' environment then there is no point attempting to trade."*

Trust in the Quality of Your Skills

As a trader it is essential to have a system fixed in your subconscious. This system must reflect an unconditional belief in your skill and viability as a trader. Trading is unstructured. Each day will be different. The only rules are those that are artificially imposed by a trading system. If you cannot trust in the way you do things then you will fail.

Relax

Nobody ever said trading was going to be easy—in fact it is often very confrontational and quite stressful. The stress that arises from trading takes a physical toll, and it is important to control this to optimise trading. There is in trading an important relationship between the psychological and the physical, however this relationship is often overlooked. If traders ignore this relationship, then trading suffers.

The way you think can be controlled consciously. It is important to be able to control the way thoughts are processed. This involves trying to control your brainwave patterns, which are related to breathing.

There are four basic brainwave patterns:

1. *Beta* is the fastest of brainwaves and is usually associated with an inability to execute complex tasks. It is linked to nervousness, panic and anxiety. Its physical manifestation is a very shallow panting-style of breathing.

2. *Alpha* is a narrow brainwave pattern associated with calmness, creativity and intuitive thinking. This style of brainwave can be stimulated by deeper, much slower abdominal breathing.

3. *Theta* is a twilight state which tends to occur when the eyes are closed just before and after sleep. It is often a state of inspiration where spontaneous solutions to problems occur.

4. *Delta* is a deep unconscious state at the bottom end of the spectrum. This can best be classified as a time of rest and regeneration.

It is obvious that traders should seek to manifest an alpha state for optimal trading. It can also be seen that a deeper form of breathing is more in tune with a trader who is in control. Traders may also want to cultivate the practice of meditation since this can act as a trigger for theta brainwave activity. It is in this state that most of the big thinking is done. Traders enter into this state without even knowing it as they watch the ebbs and flows of price action.

Fear and Anxiety Only Exist in the Past and the Future

Traders exist only in the present. This is the only time that matters to us. It is also the point in time where all trade management takes place. Some traders spend an inordinate amount of time looking back thinking of what might have been, or looking forward to what might be if the next trade comes off. Both of these timeframes are irrelevant.

All traders feel anxiety. It is natural. Markets are unstructured and we can only work with probable outcomes. Any traders who say they do not feel anxiety at some stage during the trading process are liars or fools, and both are equally dangerous. What separates the extraordinary traders from the ordinary is that the extraordinary do not let the fear of the unknown future overwhelm them.

Fear is one of the strongest of a trader's enemies since we can give our fears enough power to overwhelm us. There are three instinctive fears that present themselves to traders:

1. Fear of loss.

2. Fear of pain.

3. Fear of the unknown.

However, fear does not exist in the present—it is an anticipatory response. Traders create fear in their imagination either by looking back to previous events or by thinking forward.

Fear enters the psyche of the trader in two ways: chronic fear and acute fear.

Chronic Fear

This is more commonly referred to as worry, and it is of a relatively low intensity spread out over an extended period of time. It permeates all thoughts and actions on an everyday basis.

Chronic fear is a motivation-eater which will stifle attempts to move forward. Some of the things that traders worry about are important, however most are not and the majority are out of the control of the trader anyway. The prime source of worry for the trader is the direction of the price, and this is clearly out of the control of traders.

To combat chronic fear, drag yourself back to the present. Introspection will reveal what is troubling you.

Acute Fear

Acute fear is a tremendous impediment to the trader. It is short term and intense and can lead to a failure to act. This is the dreaded failure to pull the trigger. This can be either a failure to take an opportunity, leading to a missed future profit, or a failure to engage a stop loss, resulting in a catastrophic loss.

All traders face moments of truth. The failure to act at these times is an anticipatory reflex. The trader is anticipating a negative outcome to the action that is taken.

Combating Fear

There are a variety of simple strategies that can be engaged to combat fear:

⇒ *Centre yourself.* Realise that you are afraid but also realise that it is natural to be so. The market can be an intimidating place, particularly for the novice.

⇒ *Concentrate on the destination, not the journey.* This runs contrary to most pop spirituality babble which says that the journey and not the destination is important. This is not so in trading. The only thing that matters is the destination. If you are concerned about every minor adverse tick then you simply won't survive the journey. Focus only on the things that will cause you to bring a trade to its conclusion.

⇒ *Remember the reasons why you took up trading.* This will serve to reinvigorate you. If necessary re-live successful trades as a confidence-builder.

⇒ *Return to the present.* This is the only point in time you have control over.

If you feel the anxiety building to an intolerable level simply leave the trade. The market will still be there when you decide to return.

Dream—the Power to Imagine

When you decided to take on this most difficult of tasks and become a trader you must have had reasons for doing so. These reasons undoubtedly involved imagining what the future as a trader held for you. You dreamed of possible futures.

Dreaming is a simple child-like skill that is often lost in adulthood. My own supposition is that the rather utilitarian responsibilities of being an adult tend to grind it out of us. Being an adult has responsibilities. We have demands placed upon us and these demands are often very mundane and domestic. The life we lead is often in conflict with the life that we would have imagined for ourselves.

Successful traders have an image of themselves as successful traders. This imagery is extraordinarily important for success. It creates an unshakeable self-belief.

Optimism about the future leads to a positive expectation about events as they unfold. Pessimism, which is really a lack of dreams, breeds negative outcomes.

> *"Trading is not a hobby...You must commit to the action and lifestyle of being a trader and all that this entails."*

Traders must have the ability to believe and to dream. Believing follows a set path. Firstly the trader encounters the market. With each passing trade the belief that trading can be mastered grows. This is the beginning of establishing a set of intuitive responses that is reinforced with each encounter with the market. The second stage moves from intuitive responses to intuitive beliefs. This is the concept of faith. This is the highest level of belief. It is your belief in your ability as a trader.

However, there is a pitfall in all of this, and it is the concept of the assumed belief. This is the presumed faith based merely on what someone has told you. This is the blind faith that causes poor traders to follow tips, listen to brokers or buy a black box trading system. Worthwhile systems of belief only come out of experience.

Engage—Once the Engagement has Begun Never Look Back

Trading is not a hobby. There is no walking down the middle of the road and hoping to survive. You must commit to the action and lifestyle of being a trader and all that this entails. Trading only moves forward for the successful. Merely having blind faith is not enough.

Once you have started down the road, it is essential that you know the following to keep you headed in the right direction:

➩ *What are you seeking to accomplish?* If the target is not known how can it be hit? Know where you are going and what you are going to do when you get there.

➩ *Passion allows you to achieve.* Passion is often confused with obsession by those who lack passion themselves. Without passion you will fall at the first hurdle. The most minor of setbacks will stop you dead in your tracks.

➩ *You must have a workable plan of engagement.* All successful traders have plans to allow them to engage the market under all circumstances. No plan, no profit.

➩ *Time is not the enemy of the trader.* It does not matter whether it takes you a year or a lifetime to succeed. If your passion is strong enough then you will realise this intuitively. All great traders have had long apprenticeships.

➩ *Failures will happen.* They are inevitable and because of their inevitability you should never second-guess yourself. Hindsight is the perfect trading tool. The actions taken at any point during a trade were the actions you took—there is nothing that can be done to undo them.

Recover—Learn the Skill of Resilience

Things go wrong. Deal with it.

Taking risks by its very definition implies that failure is not only possible but likely at some point in time. This is why earlier in this chapter I stressed that it was necessary to determine your character before you began trading and to accept that loss is inevitable. If these two characteristics are in place then the journey will be easier.

Grief

When we face defeat we traditionally encounter grief. This emotion can be handled like all other emotions. It merely requires the undertaking of appropriate strategies.

The first stage in dealing with grief is to simply acknowledge that something has gone wrong. If we possess the rationality to be a trader then we will not be able to hide from what has happened. Denial is part of the arsenal of the amateur trader, not the professional. A loss is a loss and there is nothing we can do to alter this. Acceptance is the key to this first stage.

In the amateur trader denial will give way to anger. This anger will be directed at almost any inappropriate source. Amateurs become angry at their system, the advice that was taken or at the black box sitting on the desk.

Anger gives way to personal recrimination which in turn leads to self-doubt. The small voice that each of us has inside suddenly becomes much louder, eventually wearing down whatever confidence we had as traders. The voice of self-doubt then pushes us towards depression.

The final stage is acceptance. Defeats occur through a lifetime of trading. We will lose count of the number of defeats we encounter.

Part II

Money Management

"Stocks are now at what looks like a permanently high plateau."

Economist Irving Fisher, the week before the 1929 crash

4 RISK

WHAT IS THE PURPOSE of trading?

Those of you who answered *making money* are wrong. Not a little bit wrong, not a matter-of-disagreement wrong, you are catastrophically wrong. In fact you are so wrong that you have inadvertently sown the seeds of your own destruction.

In trading you only have one aim: it is *the preservation of capital. All other aims are secondary.* Nothing else matters other than holding onto your money. Some of you will disagree with this philosophy. For those who disagree consider the following equation:

$$G = \frac{L}{(1-L)} \times 100$$

G = Gain needed to recoup loss

L = Loss incurred

What this equation says is that a loss of 10% cannot be made up by a gain of 10%. For example:

$$G = \frac{0.10}{(1-0.10)} \times 100$$

$$= 11.1\%$$

If you have a trading account of $10,000 and you lose 10% then the account is down to $9,000. A gain of 10% will only take the account back to $9,900. A gain of 11.1% is necessary to take the account back to its original equity.

This simple equation leads to the following graph:

FIGURE **4.1**   **GAINS REQUIRED TO RECOVER CAPITAL**

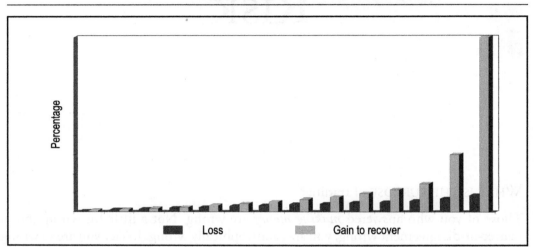

Initially this might not seem to be too extreme, but let's consider the situation of the average loss in Internet-based portfolios in the 2000 shake-out in second-tier technology stocks in the US. At the time of writing (January 2001) the average dot-com stock listed on the Nasdaq was down an average of 67% from its March 2000 price.

Let's assume that a novice trader had been unfortunate enough to be holding a dot-com that had collapsed. The gain required to get the holding back to its starting equity could be described as follows:

$$G = \frac{0.67}{(1 - 0.67)} \times 100$$

$$= 203\%$$

Therefore the trader will need to earn 203% to simply recoup this loss. Remember, this is not making a profit, merely getting the trader back to the starting point. Most traders are overly optimistic about their ability, and as such would consider this to be easy to achieve.

However, the trader will actually find this almost impossible for two reasons:

1. Such a return is simply beyond the novice, who has no idea of the practicalities and difficulties involved in trading.

2. The psychological harm that the trader has suffered from taking such a loss will have a negative impact on future trading.

If it is thought that I have been harsh in talking about the potential for losses then consider the following examples.

FIGURE 4.2   DAVNET

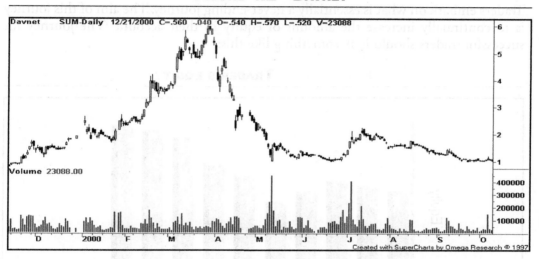

FIGURE 4.3   SAUSAGE SOFTWARE

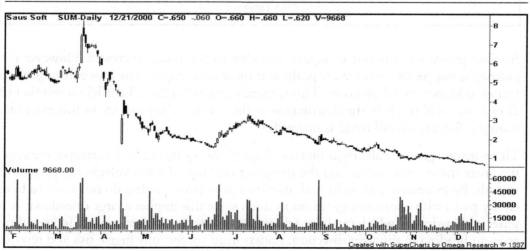

What these examples clearly demonstrate is that reward, or rather the potential for reward, can be a phantom. Once Davnet and Sausage started going down, they just kept going. It is quite possible for a trader to engage markets for years on end and never be profitable, yet every time a trader enters the market there is always risk. Many novices fall into the trap of believing that there is such a thing as a risk-less trade. This foolishness is unfortunately preyed upon by various members of the investment community, who sell so-called risk-less systems. No such thing exists.

THE NEVER-ENDING JOURNEY

Traders embark on what is essentially a never-ending journey. The aim of this journey is to continually increase the amount of equity in their account. The journey for successful traders should look something like this:

FIGURE 4.4 TRADER'S EQUITY

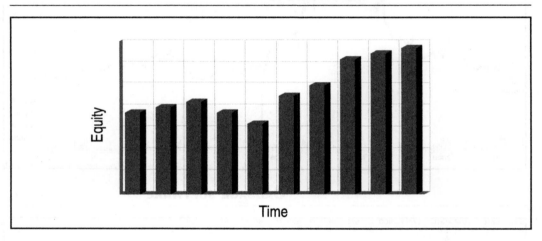

As time passes the amount of equity available to the trader increases. However the journey is not perfect—there are peaks and there are troughs. The move from peak to trough is known as a drawdown. This is merely jargon for loss. A sufficient number of drawdowns will result in the destruction of the account. You can see in this example, though, that the overall trend is upwards.

There are two general rules regarding the shape of the equity curve. The steeper the slope the faster the account grows and the straighter the slope the less volatile the pattern of growth. By extension, a straight path implies a safer path. Traders do not want to have equity paths with enormous gyrations in them since this implies a large drawdown or a series of drawdowns, which can have a disastrous impact upon the account. To keep their account heading in the right direction, traders must successfully juggle risk and reward.

Risk and Reward

True traders understand that risk is essential to trading; without risk there is no potential for reward. In all markets risk and reward are intimately bundled together. If there is no risk there is no potential for reward, therefore we need to understand and somehow quantify the risks that are faced. This process can be broken down into the following questions:

1. *What are the types of risks that are inherent in any trade?* The risks involved in trading each type of instrument will vary; for example, long-term share accumulation exposes the trader to different risks than trading commodity futures.

2. *How much risk does a trader take on each trade?* This is a pivotal concept and one that is poorly understood by traders. Research has shown that different position-sizing models can greatly alter the long-term rate of return displayed by traders.

3. *When should you leave a trade?* Your stop loss is rather like an ejector seat.

4. *Should you add additional equity to a trade?* Professional traders will only increase their exposure to the market during a profitable trade. It is only logical to add to a winning position.

Risk is the quantification of the probability and magnitude of loss based upon either one adverse event or a sequence of adverse events. Conversely, reward is the probability of, and amount to be gained from, a single or sequence of favourable events.

Traders embark upon a risk journey that largely defines how successful they will be, but if they cannot quantify risk then it is impossible to make a precise judgment about the management of the risk journey. It is fairly easy to work out reward, but remember reward can be transient—risk is ever-present. Therefore, the professional trader needs to quantify risk. To assist in this consider the following contrasting styles.

Bill and Ben

Bill and Ben are both traders. They have differing approaches to risk and its management. Bill's approach to trading is to simply buy lottery tickets for $1.00 each. Each lottery ticket he buys has a potential payoff of $10,000,000. In contrast Ben buys NCP call options for 50¢. Ben's trading methodology is such that he will exit the option if its value falls to 42¢ or if it rises to 58¢. Assume that this trade will either result in a loss of $1,000 or a gain of $1,000.

The question that needs to be asked in assessing each trade is: which of the two strategies is riskier? If we accept that the size of trading capital at risk is a reflection of the level of risk then Ben's trading strategy is riskier, since he has $1,000 at risk. The risk faced by Bill is only the $1.00 he has at risk in purchasing a lottery ticket. However, this is only part of the answer. It is necessary to quantify the probability of either Bill or Ben losing their trading capital.

If we do some simple probability analysis we can start to generate a more accurate answer to the question of which trade is riskier. The chance of Bill losing his $1.00 investment in his lottery ticket is probably 99.9999999999999%. If we assume that Ben's chance of success lies within the confines of random probability then his chance of success is 50%. On the basis of the magnitude of a loss versus the probability of a loss we therefore have a draw. Bill has the greatest potential for loss but has a lower capital exposure whereas Ben has a greater capital exposure but a higher chance of success.

However we still do not have a complete picture of who is taking the greater risk. To solve this problem we need to assume that both traders are risking the same amount of capital and that their chances of success have not altered. Their risks would then be calculated as follows:

Bill's risk = $1,000 x 0.9999999999 = $999.99

Ben's risk = $1,000 x 0.50 = $500.00

We can therefore see that, although it may initially appear that Ben is taking a greater risk, it is actually Bill who has the lesser chance of success.

Types of Risk

Professional traders define risk in two major ways. The first is avoidable risk. The second, predictably, is unavoidable risk.

Avoidable Risk

Avoidable risk is any risk that can be eliminated without any reduction in the potential for reward. An example of this would be the decision to avoid trading in very illiquid markets where in the event of an adverse move there is no chance to exit a position. Merely making the decision to trade a more liquid market removes this risk.

In a trading decision it is necessary for traders to understand the characteristics of the markets they trade. Liquidity is an essential concept for traders to understand. A small change in the criteria used to select markets can dramatically alter the risk faced. For example if faced with the opportunity to trade a highly liquid financial futures market such as the S&P500 or an emerging market index the decision as to which one to trade is obvious, and dramatically alters the trader's risk profile without altering the potential for reward.

Unavoidable Risk

The second major form of risk is unavoidable risk. This form of risk does affect the reward that can be received. If unavoidable risk is reduced then any potential for profit is also reduced.

Unavoidable risk can be further broken down into two components:

1. Controllable risk is the amount of risk that can be determined before a trade is initiated. This is determined by the trader's total risk capital as defined by the trader's position-sizing mechanism.

2. As you would anticipate the second form of unavoidable risk is known as uncontrollable risk. These are risks faced by the trader that simply cannot be quantified. Such risks can include the risk that a market may be closed or a stock suspended from trading. The most drastic form of uncontrollable risk is a serious market correction. Such corrections, whilst inevitable, are unpredictable. This form of risk is also known as market risk.

Further Sources of Risk

Here are some other sources of risk that traders should be aware of:

1. *Time*; the longer you hold a position the greater the chance for a move against you. This should not be taken as an encouragement to go out and try and day trade— such a decision could be disastrous—it is simply an attempt to get you to recognise that time and risk are linked together. All trends have what are known as counter-trend reversals. These are small moves against the prevailing trend. The longer a reversal continues the greater the chance of it becoming a fully-blown reversal.

2. *Diversification*; this is one of the least-understood areas of trading. Many believe that simply by trading differing stocks they have somehow achieved risk-reduction through diversification. This is not so. The majority of stocks show a degree of positive correlation. The only way this correlation can be avoided is by trading totally distinct instruments. For example, futures traders achieve this by trading instruments such as financial futures and a soft commodity such as orange juice or coffee. In equities markets this is difficult to achieve because of the high degree of interrelationship between stocks, particularly in tightly-packed indices such as the Twenty Leaders Index.

3. *Liquidity*; I have touched on this briefly already but it is so important that I feel the need to reiterate a few basic concepts. Poor liquidity is capable of killing traders. It is often very easy to get into a given position but sometimes virtually impossible to get out. There is an interesting dichotomy between novice traders and their more professional counterparts. Amateurs think only of buying a

given instrument, professionals wonder how easy it will be to sell out of a position in a time of crisis. This distinction becomes apparent in the desire of amateurs to trade illiquid instruments, particularly in derivatives markets. Liquidity leads to price discovery and free-flowing markets. The question needs to be asked: if nobody else wants to be in a given position what makes it so attractive that you want to be in it?

4. *Bid ask spread*; this is the difference between the price a position could be bought for versus what it could immediately be sold for. A poor bid ask spread is the result of a lack of price discovery, which is a reflection of a lack of liquidity. Traders should migrate to areas of tight bid ask spreads. This means that there are other traders in these positions.

Whilst much of this discussion regarding types of risk may seem esoteric, all concepts can be reduced to one simple concept: *trading involves risk*. Risk is merely a way of saying that there is a potential you were wrong in choosing to undertake a given trade.

Drawdowns and Systems Testing

You will remember earlier I made mention of the term 'drawdown', which is merely another term for loss. Traders need to be familiar with the term and its calculation since a never-ending sequence of drawdowns will destroy all the available equity in an account. It is also necessary to understand the term 'systems testing'. Despite being somewhat artificial a computerised systems test will give a good indication of the maximum drawdown that an account will encounter. This has ramifications for the size of a trading account since an account must be able to withstand the largest possible drawdown in order to continue to be viable.

In systems testing it is important to understand both the importance and limitation of drawdown as a measure. If for example I took a standard moving average crossover system and tested it on News Corp. (NCP) I would get a chart that gave the signals in Figure 4.5.

The up and down arrows indicate the points at which orders to go either long or short (respectively) would be placed according to the entry rules for the system. I have chosen for the sake of simplicity to only deal in single share lots, so the system has assumed that we are only trading one share at a time. I have also made this system a little simpler in that I have assumed it is either long or short, and as such it is known as a stop and reverse system. So you are either buying NCP or short selling it (see Glossary). This is a simple mechanical system that is resident within my version of SuperCharts, there is nothing special about this system, it has not even been optimised and I will explain the reasons for that in a moment.

It is also a relatively simple matter to plot an equity curve under this very rudimentary system (see Figure 4.6, opposite). This curve gives an idea of how the equity in an account would float up and down as trades were completed.

FIGURE 4.5 NEWS CORP.

FIGURE 4.6 NEWS CORP. WITH EQUITY CURVE

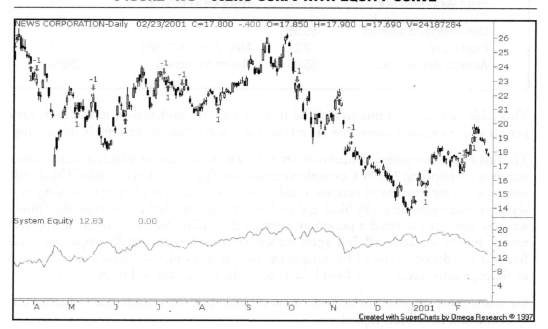

The generation of theoretical look-back trades can give you some idea as to how your system may have performed in the past. This is an important caveat; it is how it would have behaved *in the past*. Unfortunately we cannot trade the past. Exchanges are very selfish that way, they simply will not let you look at prices from six weeks ago and say I would have bought there. Nonetheless our system testing gives us some numbers that we can apply in real life.

TABLE 4.1 SYSTEMS TEST

MovAvg Crossover NEWS CORPORATION-Daily 29/03/2000 – 23/02/2001 Performance Summary: All Trades			
Total net profit	$14.75	Open position P/L	-$1.92
Gross profit	$26.93	Gross loss	-$12.18
Total # of trades	23	Percent profitable	57%
Number winning trades	13	Number losing trades	10
Largest winning trade	$8.52	Largest losing trade	-$3.62
Average winning trade	$2.07	Average losing trade	-$1.22
Ratio avg win/avg loss	1.70	Avg trade (win & loss)	$0.64
Max. consec. winners	4	Max. consec. losers	2
Avg # bars in winners	25	Avg # bars in losers	8
Max. intraday drawdown	-$5.05		
Profit factor	2.21	Max. # contracts held	1
Account size required	$5.05	Return on account	292%

This table is a simple summary of the trades that were undertaken in the look-back period and it includes some that are relevant and some that are extremely misleading.

The first figure that traders concentrate on is the return on account, which in this instance stands at a whopping 292%. Certainly a remarkable figure, but is it credible? The simple answer is *no*, for a variety of reasons. Firstly it is a very small sample we are looking at— slightly under a year. Secondly hindsight trading is always wonderfully successfully. Thirdly we may have encountered a period of wonderful trending for NCP where a stop and reverse system worked well, but again we are hampered by the small sample size. This figure is also distorted since I have made the system frictionless—I have not taken costs or slippage into account, nor have I factored in the occasional bad trade.

Of much more importance is, given certain constraints in account size, whether this system could have been traded.

You will notice that there is a line called maximum intraday drawdown. This column refers to the largest intraday dip in equity plus any losses from positions that are yet to be closed out. For this single share system this figure was $5.05, so this is the least amount of money required to trade this system. Now we have to gross up this system to see if we could actually contemplate trading it. If we are dealing in single share lots it would be simple to gross the position up by multiplying by 1,000. So if we were trading 1,000 NCP using this system we would need to be able to withstand financially and emotionally giving back $5,050 during the course of our trading. So by necessity we would need to have an account size that enables us to sleep and to continue on if we did indeed suffer such a drawdown.

However there is an extension to this idea of being able to weather a drawdown and that is: to what percentage of the account should the drawdown be limited? If on current market values we were trading 1,000 NCP a $5,050 drawdown would see us lose 27% of our capital. Such a situation would definitely be intolerable for a small account and would break every possible money management rule I could think of. The theme of under-capitalisation is one I labour constantly simply because most accounts do not have enough money in them to be viable. Despite limitations drawdown will tell you very quickly if you have enough money to trade a particular instrument.

But what if we wanted to limit the drawdown to 5% of our available capital? In such a situation we would need an account size of $100,000 to withstand this drawdown and to keep it within the acceptable limit of 5% of our equity.

As can be seen simply taking the drawdown figure from an automated systems test has serious drawbacks. Yet there is another drawback to using this figure and it relates to the nature of back-testing. Many traders make the assumption that the largest drawdown they calculate is the largest drawdown they will see. This is not so—this is merely the largest drawdown to date. Your largest drawdown may be just around the corner. Certainly analysing your trading system will give you the largest drawdown you have seen to date but it will not tell you anything about the future. Hence its utility is perhaps somewhat more limited than many believe.

The Theory of Runs

The theory of runs gives us an indication of the probability of a run of bad trades. Remember part of our definition of risk related to the probability of a string of adverse events. We need to have some idea of how many losses in a row we are likely to encounter in our trading career. The theory of runs helps us with this estimation.

Most introductions to this theory revolve around the very familiar concept of the coin toss, and I will stick with this time-honoured model. The chance of throwing either a head or a tail is ½, or 50%, each throw or trial. Each trial is regarded as being independent of every trial that came before it so it is quite possible in theory to throw ten, one hundred or even one thousand heads in a row and still have only a one-in-two chance of throwing a tail. Throughout the trial the probability of a head or a tail remains the same. This concept holds true for traders since each trade is independent of every other trade.

To illustrate this, consider the chances of throwing five heads in a row. Our probability of throwing one head is 50% so our chances are defined as follows:

Probability of throwing five heads in a row = $(0.50)^5$ = 0.03125 or 3.1%

It is important to note that the probability of throwing an additional head after this remains 50%, just as if we had just thrown 1,000 heads the probability still remains 50%.

An understanding of the theory of runs is important when considering risk.

Position Sizing

Within money management there is a pivotal concept known as 'position sizing'. Position sizing tells the trader how many of a given instrument to trade. All good traders have a methodology for deciding position sizing. The natural consequence of position sizing is that in conjunction with other factors it is designed to minimise risk whilst maximising return to the trader. It is necessary to hammer home a few facts about position sizing before going into more depth in the next chapter.

At some stage in a trader's career a series of losses will be encountered. I cannot stress too highly that a string of losses is *inevitable*. It is necessary for the trader to understand the chances of going bankrupt because of this. Professional traders recognise this inevitability and take steps to minimise its impact upon their equity.

Traders when discussing position sizing traditionally talk about a percentage risk. The percentage referred to is the percentage of their trading capital that they are willing to lose in a given trade. To illustrate in very basic terms how this works, let's assume that instead of tossing a coin the trader has a system that is right 50% of the time. What are the chances of this system being wrong five times in a row? The answer is 0.03125, or slightly over 3.1%. This may seem small, but it is quite possible to have five losing trades in a row.

The important question is: how will this rather abstract number affect traders and their ability to survive? Let's assume that a trader has a $100,000 float and is risking $20,000 per trade. According to the theory of runs the trader has a 3% chance of losing everything (if we assume the chance of success for each trade is 50%). This is unlikely to happen however, because the trader would quit long before the final loss due to the psychological distress of losing the majority of the account. After three losing trades, this account would be down 60%. From this point recovery is almost impossible.

> *"A simple change in the capital at risk will dramatically alter the risk of ruin."*

By now the astute reader will be starting to understand the importance of risk management. If the scenario of having a 3% chance of losing all of a trading float is too high the question then becomes: how can the risk be lowered? A simple change in the capital at risk will dramatically alter the risk of ruin. If instead of risking $20,000 per trade the trader decides to risk $10,000 then the risk of ruin becomes as follows:

Probability of ruin = $9.76 \times (10)^{-14}$

By simply halving the capital at risk the trader has dramatically altered the risk of ruin.

The 2% Rule

Traditionally traders talk in terms of the 2% rule, which means that they are only willing to risk 2% of their capital in any given trade. For example, if a trader has a $100,000 trading float then the trader is initially willing to commit 2% of this trading float to each position undertaken. It does not mean that the trader will only commit $2,000 to each trade. This is a misconception held by many novice traders. The 2% rule is just the first step in sizing a position properly. If a trade goes in the right direction, then the trader can add to the trade (see page 66—'When to Buy More'). If the trade goes south then the trader has only lost the 2%.

To consider the relevance of the 2% rule see how the theory of runs applies to a $100,000 account that is being traded using a system that is correct 50% of the time. To lose the entire $100,000 account a trader using the 2% rule would need to be wrong 50 times in a row. The probability of this is defined as follows:

Probability of ruin = $(0.50)^{50} = 8.88 \times 10^{-16}$

This is as small a number as most people are likely to encounter in their lives. It is easiest to think of this number as effectively being zero.

Many novice traders think that the 2% rule was simply plucked out of the air or is used by traders who simply do not have the nerve to place at risk large amounts of their trading capital, but it should be remembered that there are old traders and bold traders. There are no old bold traders.

The rule is simple: *the more you risk, the greater your chance of ruin. The less you risk the greater your chance of survival.*

This understanding will greatly assist the trader. However, it is only the first step in defining risk. The 2% rule is merely a broad guide to how much risk to accept. It does not give a complete understanding of position sizing. Traders need to decide how much of their trading capital should be allocated to each position. The answer to this can be found in applying commonsense and an intuitive understanding of the theory of runs.

We will use as an example the following equity curves, which have been built up by trading simulations. The rules for the generation of these curves are very simple. The initial account size is $50,000, it is assumed that the trading system is correct 40% of the time and it has a 2:1 profit-to-loss ratio; effectively for every dollar lost in an unsuccessful trade two dollars are made in each successful trade.

FIGURE 4.7   10% CAPITAL IN EACH TRADE (2:1 PROFIT-TO-LOSS)

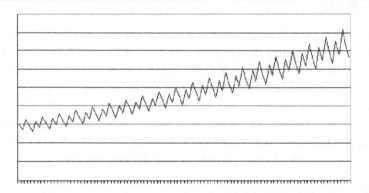

FIGURE 4.8   15% CAPITAL IN EACH TRADE (2:1 PROFIT-TO-LOSS)

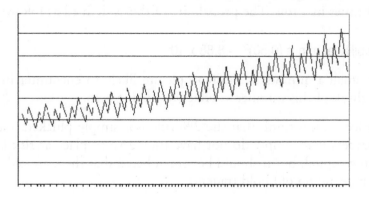

FIGURE 4.9   25% CAPITAL IN EACH TRADE (2:1 PROFIT-TO-LOSS)

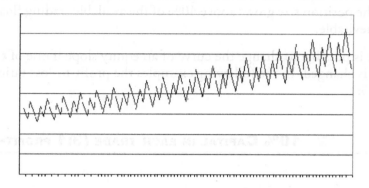

FIGURE 4.10   40% CAPITAL IN EACH TRADE (2:1 PROFIT-TO-LOSS)

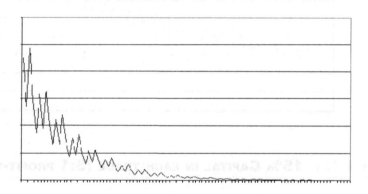

FIGURE 4.11   50% CAPITAL IN EACH TRADE (2:1 PROFIT-TO-LOSS)

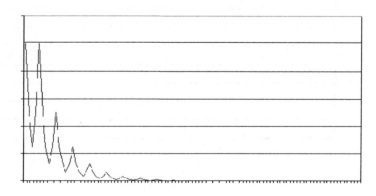

As can be seen the larger the percentage of capital allocated to a trade the greater the oscillations in the equity curve and the greater the risk of ruin. From this it is obvious that once the position size grows above 40% of the available trading float then disaster becomes inevitable.

However it is possible to change the curve of an equity slope if one of the variables in the system is changed. In the following examples the profit-to-loss ratio of the system is lifted to 3:1.

FIGURE 4.12   10% CAPITAL IN EACH TRADE (3:1 PROFIT-TO-LOSS)

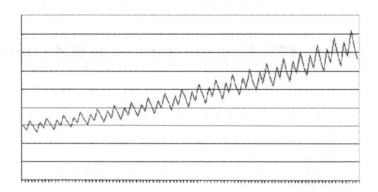

FIGURE 4.13   15% CAPITAL IN EACH TRADE (3:1 PROFIT-TO-LOSS)

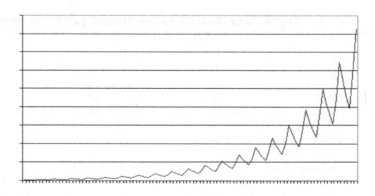

FIGURE 4.14   25% CAPITAL IN EACH TRADE (3:1 PROFIT-TO-LOSS)

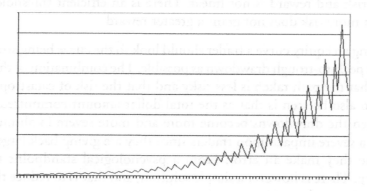

FIGURE 4.15   40% CAPITAL IN EACH TRADE (3:1 PROFIT-TO-LOSS)

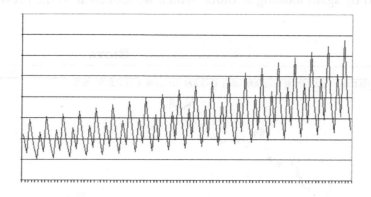

FIGURE 4.16   50% CAPITAL IN EACH TRADE (3:1 PROFIT-TO-LOSS)

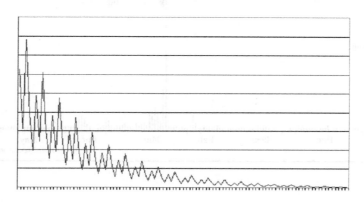

What these equity curves more than adequately demonstrate is that the relationship between risk and reward is not linear. There is an efficient threshold beyond which taking on more risk does not grant a greater reward.

In assessing an equity curve a trader should look to the curve being straight and having as small a peak-to-trough drawdown as possible. The combination of these two elements implies that the path taken is less risky and that the risk of catastrophic loss is lower. What can also be seen is that as the total dollar amount committed to one position grows then the drawdowns become more and more severe in absolute dollar terms. This has a severe impact upon traders since they are giving back large sums of money each time they make an error. From a psychological standpoint this can be very distressing. There is however a simple solution, and that is to reduce the level of equity committed to each position even further.

There is a commonsense reason for keeping position sizes relatively small and it can be illustrated by again looking at Biota (which we looked at in the previous chapter).

FIGURE 4.17 BIOTA

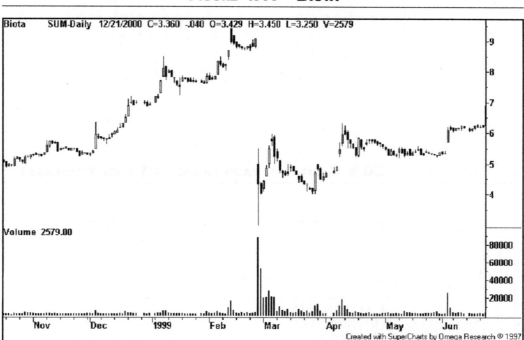

Eventually Biota did recover but that can only be seen with the benefit of hindsight. If you had 40% of your capital in a position and it declined by 60% then your trading float would be down by 24%. To recover from this would require a gain of 31% to get back to the initial level of equity.

There is above all the mathematics of money management a simple maxim: if you cannot sleep at night because of your exposure to the market then you are risking too much money.

5 POSITION SIZING EXPLORED

THERE IS A SIMPLE RULE TO DO with position sizing; if you do not understand what the term 'position sizing' refers to stop trading immediately. It is often very interesting to ask novice traders about position sizing. It is a concept that immediately separates the professional from the amateur.

In examining position sizing I will look at three models. The first—the equal portions model—is fairly simple and widely accepted. The second and third models—the percentage risk model and the volatility model—look to use risk as the basis for setting position size.

1. The Equal Portions Model

This is a method familiar to all market participants. It is based upon dividing your capital into equal portions and then purchasing baskets of shares. In such a model you may have $100,000 equity and decide to split this into ten lots of $10,000.

This creates the illusion that you are undertaking some form of diversification and hence risk control. The illusion of diversification comes from the fact that the shares purchased have different names. The thinking goes, particularly among brokers, that if your shares have different names then you are not exposed to market risk, therefore you have engaged in a risk-reduction exercise. Such thinking is flawed because all equities are correlated, and the major risk traders are exposed to is market risk.

There is an advantage with this model in that it is very simple and quite intuitive, and the risk that is faced by the trader is even across the portfolio. However it has some major disadvantages. It assumes that risk should be even across the various instruments, irrespective of the underlying volatility of the individual instrument. This is a dangerous assumption since it is quite possible that you may enter a position when the associated risk is very high. Most importantly there is no attempt to set a limit to the risk that is faced on the initial entry to a position.

2. The Percentage Risk Model

This model revolves around setting a percentage of total capital that a trader is willing to risk and then sizing the trade accordingly. It needs to be stressed that the percentage risk is not the amount that will be put into each position. This is a common misconception and a sign of a tremendous misunderstanding of how this or any other position-sizing model works. What the percentage risk defines is the risk that will be accepted by the trader when a position is entered.

To illustrate how this works assume that a trader is using a breakout trading system to trade BHP and that the signal to buy has been generated at $19.00, and that the trader will exit the trade should the price slip to $18.00. Assume the trader is starting with $100,000 and using 2% risk.

To decide how many shares will be purchased the trader divides the initial risk ($2,000) by the loss resulting from a presumed exit at $18.00 ($1.00 loss). The number of BHP shares that can be purchased is: $2,000/$1.00 = 2,000 shares. At the purchase price of $19.00 this equates to $38,000 worth, or 38% of available trading funds. This may be considered to be an excessive amount to place in one position and as a consequence it can be seen why many traders cut their initial risk back to 1%, since this would drop the position exposure to $19,000.

> *"What the percentage risk defines is the risk that will be accepted by the trader when a position is entered."*

In deciding how to set an exit point traders may use a line of support or a last major low. It is important though that once this is decided it is adhered to. Consider the following chart of IXL (see Figure 5.1, opposite). The volatility-based entry system I use gave a buy signal on 16 August for entry the next morning. For this trade the most logical place to engage a stop would be just below the zone of congestion at $1.00, since a close below this level would indicate a breach of support and a high probability of a move down to the bottom of the congestion zone at 95¢. Therefore it would be sensible to place the stop at 98¢, which is just below the line of support.

FIGURE 5.1 IXL

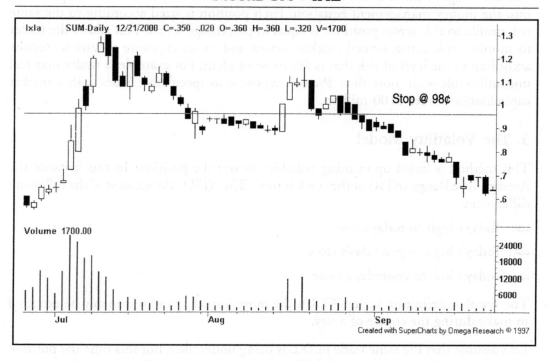

From here it is possible to start getting an idea of how to size this position. If we assume a total equity of $50,000 and accept a risk of 1% and that a position was entered into the next morning when price opened at $1.09, then the size of the position would be as follows:

Stop loss point for entry = 98¢

Entry price = $1.09

Risk premium = $500 (1% of $50,000)

Position size = $500/(Entry – Stop loss)

= $500/11¢

= 4,545 shares can be purchased

Total exposure at entry price of $1.09 = $4,954 (excluding brokerage)

At the time of writing IXL is drifting, which would necessitate the implementation of a time stop (see following chapter) to avoid being caught in any congestion.

The advantage of this method is that it introduces the concept of a fixed risk premium into the money management equation. Each position is sized according to the same risk profile so risk across positions is equal in percentage terms. This allows the trader to monitor risk across several market sectors and to set exposure to various sectors according to the level of risk that is felt to be prudent. For example, a trader may feel uncomfortable with more than 3% risk exposure to speculative issues with a market capitalisation under $100 million.

3. The Volatility Model

This method is based upon using volatility to size the position. In this instance the Average True Range (ATR) of the stock is used. The ATR is the greatest of the following differences:

⇔ Today's high to today's low

⇔ Today's high to yesterday's close

⇔ Today's low to yesterday's close.

The simplest definition is that ATR is the move a stock could reasonably be expected to make during the course of a day.

Let's assume that the same trade in IXL is being undertaken but this time the position is sized using the volatility model. To size this position the following calculation is undertaken:

ATR (20 day) = 7.5¢

Entry price = $1.09

Risk premium = $500 (1% of $50,000)

Position size = $500/(2ATR)

= $500/15¢

= 3,333 shares can be purchased.

Total exposure at entry price of $1.09 = $3,633 (excluding brokerage)

The reason why 2ATR was chosen instead of 1ATR is because in a system using volatility as both the entry signal and the position-sizing methodology then an exit system using volatility should also be used. In this instance an exit of two ATR will be used. (The concept of exits based upon ATR will be looked at in the next chapter.)

This methodology is built upon the basis that risk and exposure across various instruments is equalised by risk management. Using this system it is difficult for a trader to take a greater loss than has already been predefined.

Futures Trading

The great advantage of this model is in its application to futures trading. Consider a trader with a $50,000 trading float and a 1% risk threshold who trades the Share Price Index contract. The ATR of the SPI is 35 points (at the time of writing). Each point equals $25.00 so the ATR value is $875.00. To size this position the risk threshold is divided by the value of the ATR: $500/$875 = 0.57. Clearly it is impossible to trade 0.57 of a futures contract so at this risk level this trade must be ignored. At the

> *"...volatility-based methodology...forces the trader to reduce the level of risk if it has a disproportionate impact upon the trading account..."*

time of writing accepting a 1% risk level and an ATR of 35 points a trader would need $87,500 to trade a single SPI contract. Clearly this provides an impediment to the various SPI trading schemes that some spruikers insist you can open with only $10,000.

This is the beauty of the volatility-based methodology—it forces the trader to reduce the level of risk if it has a disproportionate impact upon the trading account, hence the chance of a catastrophic loss obliterating the bulk of the equity in an account is dramatically reduced.

MULTIPLE POSITIONS

The position-sizing examples I have used so far have been based around single positions. Whilst most amateurs have single-stock portfolios, traders will engage the market with multiple positions, hence any position-sizing tool that is used must take into account this fact. There are two approaches that can be adopted—these are traditionally referred to as the core equity model and the total equity model.

The Core Equity Model

The core equity model assumes that as each position is added then the risk premium of this position is subtracted from the total equity. For example, if the trader has a float of $100,000 and has a risk premium of 1% then this 1% ($1,000) is subtracted from the trading float for the purposes of sizing the next position. So if another position is added and the risk premium of 1% is maintained then the risk exposure is 1% of $99,000, or $990.00.

The Total Equity Model

The total equity model makes the assumption that the available capital to trade is composed of the cash balance plus any open profit. If a trader has $95,000 in cash and an open position with a market value of $17,000 then the total available equity to trade would be $112,000. So if a new position were to be opened and the 1% risk premium rule adhered to, the new risk premium would be $1,120 based upon 1% of the total value of the available equity.

Naturally the mechanism that is used will determine the rate of growth of equity in any given account. The total equity model will result in greater growth since the position size will always be a reflection of unrealised profits and available cash.

When I examine pyramiding (see page 66) I will look at the impact of both methods on a trade and the rate of growth that can be achieved using each model.

Position-Sizing Maintenance

Markets fluctuate. The equity value of an account ebbs and flows as the market moves. With this fluctuation in mind it is necessary to monitor the exposure of each position to the market on an ongoing basis; for equities traders this may only be done once a week, for futures traders it may be done on a constant daily market-to-market basis.

As an example consider the following trade in Santos (STO). Assume that risk is going to be monitored on a weekly basis, and kept constant at 1%. Assume that the following conditions are in effect:

Trading float = $250,000

Entry price = $4.05

Risk premium = 1%

ATR = 12¢

Risk premium at 1% = $250,000/1%

$$= \$2,500$$

Position size = $2,500/24¢

$$= 10,416 \text{ shares @ } \$4.05$$

$$= \$42,184.80$$

At the end of week one of the trade the risk profile of the trade is reviewed:

Current market price = $4.65

Current market value = $48,434.40

$ change in position = $6,249.60

Total trading equity = $256,249.60

As the trade has progressed a two bar trailing stop has been employed (see Chapter 6 for more information on stop losses). At the time of the risk review this stop is at $4.40. If this stop is hit then the position will be liquidated for a total equity of $45,830. However in the initial position-sizing calculation it was stated that risk would be maintained at 1%. At the current value of the position 1% is $2,562.49. The current open risk is 1.45%, or $3,645.60. This is calculated as the difference between the amount of equity that would be generated by having the stop hit at $4.40 and the initial equity committed to the position, i.e. $45,830.40 − $42,184.80. Hence the trade size would need to be recalculated to bring the position back into line with the already predetermined level of risk. To achieve this $1,083.11 worth of STO would have to be sold.

Whilst this may initially appear a little complicated for traders who are new to position sizing all that is being done is making certain the risk for this position does not creep beyond the set 1% level. Whenever the open risk exceeds 1%, equity will need to be reduced to bring the position back into line. Position sizing is not only about how many of any given instrument a trader is allowed to buy but how many to keep.

Capital Allocation Models

It should be noted that position sizing is not capital allocation—the two are remarkably different concepts and they are often confused with one another. Position sizing tells you how many of a given instrument will be purchased and held. Capital allocation tells you what sector of the market or markets you will allocate capital to. I alluded to this earlier when I stated that a trader might not be comfortable with more than 3% risk exposure to shares with a market capitalisation of under $100 million.

A capital allocation model for a share trader may be along the following lines:

Stocks with a market capitalisation < $100 million: 2% exposure.

Stocks with a market capitalisation of $100 million to $500 million: 2% exposure.

Stocks with a market capitalisation > $500 million: 1% exposure.

Please note this is not a model to be followed, merely an example of what can be done.

Diversification

In equities trading it is difficult to achieve diversification because of the interrelationship of stocks, particularly if a trader has confined activity to the top 20. As would be expected each of these stocks displays a high degree of correlation, so to expect this style of portfolio to be insulated against any form of downturn in the broad market is unrealistic. This problem is compounded since it has been found that the bulk of portfolios are single-stock portfolios. To a degree this problem of a lack of diversification is offset by having a risk-based position-sizing methodology and by seeking to minimise the risks that were outlined earlier in the section on avoidable risk.

Simply buying different stocks does not produce true diversification. The only way to really diversify is to undertake either one or preferably all of the following approaches:

1. Trade multiple timeframes

Traders should seek to engage the market over many timeframes, ranging from short—one to three days—to long—timeframes involving trading weekly signals.

2. Trade multiple markets

This will involve traders undertaking additional work. It is the prime risk-reduction and diversification mechanism undertaken by futures traders. However do not fall into the trap of, for example, believing you have diversified because you have bought a portfolio of shares and have then gone long the SPI. This approach should involve, for example, being long Australian shares, short the FTSE via a call option play and long the $US via a managed currency fund or simply buying traveller's cheques. Such a methodology also satisfies the criteria of point one (above).

> *"Simply buying different stocks does not produce true diversification."*

3. Trade multiple money management systems

It is quite possible to trade a single account using a variety of money management approaches. There is no rule that says you cannot trade a variety of position-sizing vehicles, each with different pyramiding and exit strategies.

4. Trade multiple systems

Two points should be obvious to the astute reader by now. There is no Holy Grail, and markets change in tone and character. It is therefore only logical to have two systems. I am not talking about continually trying to make up your trading as you go along but rather to have two separate approaches. My own approach is made up of two separate triggers that are traded in two separate ways. The first trigger is volatility-based, the second is based on traditional technical analysis, where I build a picture in my mind of how I perceive the market.

5. Scan using multiple criteria

One of the great tests for traders is how information is managed. Many novice traders are extremely inefficient in the way they view the market—they are terrified of missing out on the next big thing. As a result their psyche is buffeted by so many inputs they simply are either unable to take in all the information they are presented with or they are unable to make a decision based upon this information.

Scanning the market should be done mechanically. Criteria that could be used may include any or all of the following:

- Price and volume breakouts.
- Divergences.
- Range expansions.
- Pattern recognition.
- Relative strength comparisons.

This list is by no means exhaustive and is only limited by your imagination.

6. Limit your trading

It might seem to be a paradox to tell you to limit your trading in a book about trading, but this is actually a risk control mechanism and form of psychological diversification.

Most people who are new to markets believe that trading is a wild chaotic endeavour where decisions must be made hourly. Unfortunately for all of you reading this book in the hope of being a highly-aggressive intraday trader your chances of success are virtually zero. The overwhelming body of evidence is that frequent trading actually reduces a trader's performance. Once again the evidence for this comes from the work by Odean. In a study of 78,000 households in the US he found that average traders turned over approximately 75% of their portfolio annually. In his study, a turnover of 70% earned an average net return that was 3.7% less than an index of NYSE–Nasdaq–AMEX stocks. By trading more often the vast majority of traders will guarantee that they will earn less than the prevailing market rate of return—the greater the rate of turnover the greater the underperformance.

This is not an argument for a rather mundane and incredibly ineffective strategy of buy and hold, but rather a warning against the dangers of overtrading. Trade only when you are confident that the money is there for the taking. As I write this book the market is in an extreme state of flux and is very difficult to trade. As a professional I recognise this and have stepped out of the market. Recognise that you do not have to be in the market all the time. Choose your moments very carefully.

When to Buy More (Pyramiding)

To date I have concentrated on the simple concepts of position sizing and the need for control of risk. The importance of these two areas cannot be underestimated, but there is another arm to the broad concept of money management. This concept revolves around what is known as 'pyramiding'. Pyramiding is adding to an already existing profitable position. It is also known as averaging up.

Before I continue I need to issue a warning. Under *no* circumstances do you ever average down. *Never* buy more of a share that has breached your stop loss points. Averaging down is a strategy employed by fools. Averaging up is a strategy used by professionals.

Pyramiding Strategies

Pyramiding is the sequential addition of capital to a position that is heading in the trader's favour. This can be done either using fixed targets or by adding once lines of resistance have been breached. It is based upon the concept of traders becoming risk-seeking when the trend is heading in their direction (see Chapter 2). Unfortunately this is extraordinarily difficult for traders to achieve, and that is why it is the hallmark of the professional trader.

I have already referred to the concept of ATR position sizing, however ATR can also be used to set landmarks to guide in adding to positions.

In this example using Davnet (DVT—see Figure 5.2, opposite) the trade will be pyramided in over three trades, beginning with 50% of the original position size at entry. This is then followed up with two staggered entries of 25%, at entry plus 2ATR and entry plus 4ATR. This is a sequential entry into a trade. (It is also known as legging in.)

The following are the salient points of this trade:

Trading float = $100,000

Risk premium = 1%

Entry signal = $1.20

ATR @ entry = 11¢

Staggered entry = price @ entry + 2ATR and price @ entry + 4ATR

Entries @ $1.20; $1.42; $1.64

Position size = $1,000/22¢ = 4,545 shares

FIGURE 5.2 DAVNET

If this were to be a single entry then all 4,545 shares would be purchased at $1.20, but this is a staggered entry so the trenches are as follows:

Initial = 2,272 shares @ $1.20

Second = 1,136 shares @ $1.42

Final = 1,136 shares @ $1.64

There is a subtlety in this style of pyramiding that needs to be examined more closely. Notice how the final two trenches are unequal with respect to the level of capital allocated. The second entry is $1,613.12 compared to the final entry of $1,863.04. The level of equity committed to each position has begun to drift upwards. This should not be a problem since it is merely a minor variation on the total equity model of position sizing, whereby advantage is taken of the growth in the underlying total value of the combined trading float.

There is however a second way of viewing this style of staggered entry, and that is to resize the positions based upon the prevailing ATR. The basic technique of the trade is identical; an initial commitment followed by two additional staggered entries, each one rescaled at the time of entry.

The trade therefore becomes the following:

Initial = \$500/(2ATR @ entry) = \$500/22¢ = 2,272 shares, or \$2,726.40

Second = \$250/(2ATR @ entry) = \$250/30¢ = 833 shares, or \$1,182.86

Final = \$250/(2ATR @ entry) = \$250/32¢ = 781 shares, or \$1,280.84

This method simply recalibrates the capital commitment based upon the prevailing ATR. This helps keep the risk at the predetermined risk level. However it does not take into account any periodic risk maintenance that the trader may wish to conduct.

Re-entry

The previous example dealt with the sequential introduction of capital into a new position. However it is possible to find a situation whereby a position has continued to run after the full commitment has been made. In such a situation a re-entry signal may be established and additional capital committed to the trade.

If we revisit the Davnet chart these potential points for re-entry can be seen as the stock makes small counter-trend reversals. These reversals provide the opportunity to re-enter a position and lift the level of equity committed to the position.

FIGURE 5.3   DAVNET

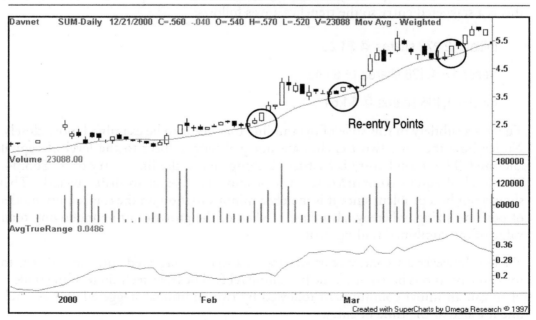

I will examine these triggers using both the core equity and the total equity models. I will assume both models take the same triggers and the same exit.

Pyramiding Using the Core Equity Model

In this method the risk premium for each leg into a stock is subtracted from the original trading capital and positions resized accordingly:

Trading float = $100,000

Risk premium = 2.5%

Initial trigger = $2.43

ATR = 18¢

Initial position = $2,500/36¢

= 6,944 shares or $16,873.92

The second re-entry trigger comes as DVT closes on the moving average but fails to penetrate. This is a fairly common re-entry signal. It yields the following position sizing protocol:

Trading float = $97,500 (note the float has been recalculated to take account of the existing position)

Risk premium = 1.5% (lowered to reduce risk)

Trigger = $3.80

ATR = 24¢

Second position = $1,462.50/48¢

= 3,046 shares or $11,574.80

The final position is triggered at $4.94:

Trading float = $96,037.50

Risk premium = 1.0%

Trigger = $4.94

ATR = 34¢

Final position = $960.37/68¢

= 1,412 shares or $6,975.28

This trade can be summarised as follows:

Total number of shares purchased = 11,402

Total capital committed to position = $35,424.00

Capital return assuming an exit at $6.00 = $68,412.00

Profit = $32,988.00

There are a few points that need to be highlighted. Firstly the risk premium in each new trade was scaled back to further reduce risk. Secondly there was no recognition made of the upward drift in capital allocation. Each trade has simply been taken as a new trade. Finally under no circumstances would a trader commit 35% of the total trade float to a single trade. This clearly violates the capital allocation models that were referred to earlier. It does not matter whether each pyramid is regarded as a new trade or simply an addition to an existing trade; 35% of capital in one instrument defies reason. This however does not mean that we do not take advantage of the ability to pyramid that long-running trends present us with, it simply means that we exercise that rarest of resources—common sense.

To lower the risk in pyramiding a trader may simply rescale the risk premium. In this example the risk premium dropped from 2.5% to 1.5%, and then to 1.0% as the final decision to pyramid was taken. A risk-averse trader may even decide to scale back the exposure to new positions even more savagely than I have done.

Pyramiding Using the Total Equity Model

The second method of pyramiding into a trade utilises the total equity model. I will demonstrate the functioning of this model by using the same trade. The trade starts with the same methodology as the core equity model:

Trading float = $100,000

Risk premium = 2.5%

Initial trigger = $2.43

ATR = 18¢

Initial position = $2,500/36¢

= 6,944 shares or $16,873.92

The difference starts to emerge with the second leg of the pyramid, triggered at $3.80:

Trading float = $83,126.08 + 6,944 DVT @ $3.80 with market value of $26,387.20

Total float = $109,513.28

Risk premium = 1.5%

Trigger = $3.80

ATR = 24¢

Second position = $1,642.60/48¢

= 3,422 shares or $13,003.60

The final position is triggered at $4.94:

Trading float = $70,122.48 + 10,366 DVT @ $4.94 with a market value of $51,208.04

Total float = $121,330.52

Risk premium = 1.0%

Trigger = $4.94

ATR = 34¢

Final position = $1,213.30/68¢

= 1,784 or $8,812.96

This trade can be summarised as follows:

Total number of shares purchased = 12,150

Total capital committed to position = $38,690.48

Capital return assuming an exit at $6.00 = $72,900.00

Profit = $34,209.52

Notice how the capital exposure in this model is higher compared to the core equity model, however the risk exposure is the same as that of the core equity model. The difference, as would be expected, is in the use of the unrealised profits to bolster the size of the trading float. This leads to greater overall capital exposure and an extremely high growth in equity.

However it should be noted that the need for protective profit stops in this model is paramount since the trader is using an unrealised gain to dramatically increase exposure to the market. This methodology will only work if the trader is highly disciplined in the use of stops to protect equity.

71

Conclusion

In closing this section on money management I need to highlight the two vital maxims of risk control. Firstly, use your brain. Over the years I have found that novice traders have an intuitive understanding of risk control. This understanding is based upon experience from everyday life. When it comes to trading, however, this experience seems to go straight out the window as traders take on all the hallmarks of the gambling trader. Secondly, you must be able to sleep at night. If you are uncomfortable with the size of a position merely scale back the risk to a point you are comfortable with.

> *"...I need to highlight the two vital maxims of risk control. Firstly, use your brain...Secondly, you must be able to sleep at night."*

6   STOP LOSSES

THE MOST IMPORTANT ASPECT OF money management—position sizing—has already been addressed. Please do not do what most amateurs do, and that is confuse stop losses with a comprehensive approach to money management. (Even then most amateurs get it wrong by not even adhering to their stops.)

Having said this, stop losses are an integral part of money management. A stop loss may be defined as any tool that causes traders to exit a position when it is perceived that the position has moved against them. Stop losses fall into a variety of categories, and we will look at each of these individually.

Hard or Initial Stop

This stop is engaged the instant a position is entered and is related to the position-sizing methodology. For example if you were using a volatility-based position-sizing tool which is based upon 2ATR then the initial stop would be 2ATR from entry. In the earlier IXL example an ATR of 7.5¢ was calculated and the hard stop would be: entry price – 2ATR.

As a further example assume that we had entered a position in National (NAB) at $24.50 using a position-sizing methodology based upon 2ATR, and at the time of entry the 20-day ATR was 42.9¢ (which we round up to 43¢). The hard or initial stop for this position would be: $24.50 – 86¢ = $23.64 (see Figure 6.1, overleaf).

FIGURE 6.1   **NAB** INITIAL OR HARD STOP

If a percentage-risk model is used then the point from which the percentage risk was calculated would naturally be the initial stop. If your position sizing were based upon a line of support or a significant low then this would be the point at which the stop would be placed.

The stops placed on entry must be adhered to since positions generally go wrong shortly after entry.

Breakeven Stop

When a position is entered the hard stop is engaged. As the market moves up this stop is moved to the level at which the position was entered. This enables the trader to exit the market at breakeven should the position reverse suddenly in its early stages. All stops should be moved to breakeven at the earliest opportunity. In the above example the initial stop was $23.64. The position was entered into at $24.50 so the breakeven stop would be $24.50.

One of the hardest questions faced by traders is: when should the initial stop be moved to the breakeven stop? There are a variety of methodologies for this. They include moving the stop to breakeven at entry plus 2ATR. This is quite logical when positions are entered gradually and the first pyramid is set at 2ATR. If a percentage-loss methodology is used then the initial stop is moved to breakeven when the stock price moves to two times the amount of give-back the trader had anticipated. For example, if the trader had placed the initial stop at $1.00 and had then entered the stock at

$1.10 the amount of give-back is 10¢, so the stop would be moved to breakeven when the price had moved to $1.30, which is entry plus two times the initial give-back. If the trader uses a stop loss system based upon a number of trailing bars then the initial stop would be moved to breakeven after a set number of bars.

Trailing or Profit Stop

This style of stop is used as a profit-protection method. As the amount of profit in a trade increases this stop moves in tandem with it. There are a variety of subsets of the trailing profit stop, including:

1. *The dollar or percentage stop*

    This stop is built around the concept that the trader is willing to give back a certain dollar or percentage amount before quitting a position.

    However it is important to note that these stops must be fluid in their application. For example imagine that NCP is being traded and the position is entered at $20.00. The profit stop is set at 30% of the profit from entry. If NCP climbs to $22.00 the trader is willing to give back 60¢; if it climbs to $24.00 then $1.20 would be given back before exiting the market. If NCP were to climb to $30.00 then $3.00 would be given back before the position were to be shut down.

    As NCP climbed, the dollar amount that the trader was willing to lose became greater and greater because of the rigid fixed-percentage amount that was placed at risk. As the dollar amount of a profit increases the percentage at risk should be decreased to avoid giving back too much profit.

2. *Technical stops*

    It is also possible for this style of stop to be based upon a technical indicator such as the breach of a trendline or the puncturing of a moving average. An example of the application of a moving average can be seen in Figure 6.2 (overleaf). Some possible exit signals are highlighted.

    In this example an 18-day weighted moving average could be used as a simple stop and reverse technique. Such a technique can be said to be self-correcting because the stop is the buy or sell signal and will allow the trader to reverse the direction of the trade.

    Such a method can also be employed using a simple trendline. For example Sausage (see Figure 6.3, overleaf) is a stock that can be legally short sold (see Glossary for an explanation of short selling). If a short sale had been opened at the reversal from $3.29 then a simple trendline could serve as the trailing stop.

    Another popular mechanical method is known as the Parabolic SAR (Stop And Reverse). The Parabolic SAR is so-named because it resembles a parabola as it is plotted.

FIGURE 6.2   CRB

FIGURE 6.3   SAUSAGE

It was originally designed to fulfil the need for a mechanical trend-following stop. During the early stages of the trade the stop is quite wide, thereby giving price room to manoeuvre. As the trend accelerates the stop moves closer to the zone of price action.

3. *Volatility-based stop*

This has already been touched on in the discussion on hard or initial stops. The concept of ATR may also be used to set a trailing stop that is based upon a set ATR-based retrenchment from a high. Such a stop has the following appearance. Some possible signals are highlighted, depending on whether you were short or long.

FIGURE 6.4 VOLATILITY-BASED STOP

4. *Profit stop*

This stop engages when a certain amount of profit has been achieved. It is simply the setting of a target price based upon whatever criteria are chosen. Once the target is achieved the position is liquidated.

Time Stop

Congestion is the enemy of the directional trader; as such it needs to be avoided. This type of situation may be encountered when a trader perceives that a stock has bounced off a level of support but failed to move ahead. This stop is engaged if the stock fails to move ahead by a set percentage by a given time. The concept of ATR can also be used; for example, if the stock fails to move 2ATR from the entry point by a given time, the position would be exited. Or if the stock failed to move 1ATR plus the high of the day on which the position was entered then the trade would be wound up.

> *"The rule for stops is simple; no stops, no survival. The market will always give you a chance to get out."*

Psychological Stop

Initially I hesitated from including this form of stop in this review of exit methodologies for fear that the novice would regard it as an argument for not placing stops. It is nothing of the sort. It is merely a recognition that some traders have a wonderful intuitive feel for the market and will act according to this intuition. Intuitive traders have stops that are just as concrete as those discussed, it is just that their application is a reflection of their own approach to the market.

The rule for stops is simple; no stops, no survival. The market will always give you a chance to get out.

Conclusion

For those who doubt the importance of money management consider the following fact. A study by Brinson, Singer and Beebower titled *Determinants of Portfolio Performance 11* (published in the *Financial Analyst's Journal 47,* May–June 1991, pp 40–49) found that in a group of 82 large pension funds, 91.5% of the variance in their returns could be explained by their differing money management strategies. The timing and choice of investment vehicle accounted for less than 10% of their returns.

For those of you who still doubt the importance of money management I will leave the last word to some of the world's greatest traders:

> *"[Michael Marcus, another top trader] taught me one other thing that is absolutely critical: You have to be willing to make mistakes regularly; there is nothing wrong with it. Michael taught me about making your best judgement, being wrong, making your next best judgement, being wrong, making your third best judgement, and then doubling your money."* – **Bruce Kovner**

> *"You should always have a worst case point. The only choice should be to get out quicker."* – **Richard Dennis**

"That cotton trade was almost the deal breaker for me. It was at that point that I said, 'Mr. Stupid, why risk everything on one trade? Why not make your life a pursuit of happiness rather than pain?'" – **Paul Tudor Jones**

"If I have positions going against me, I get right out; if they are going for me, I keep them...Risk control is the most important thing in trading. If you have a losing position that is making you uncomfortable, the solution is very simple: get out, because you can always get back in." – **Paul Tudor Jones**

"Don't focus on making money; focus on protecting what you have." – **Paul Tudor Jones**

"Ninety-five per cent of my profits have come from five per cent of my trades." – **Richard Dennis**

"Throughout my financial career, I have continually witnessed examples of other people that I have known being ruined by a failure to respect risk. If you don't take a hard look at risk, it will take you." – **Larry Hite**

"Frankly, I don't see markets; I see risks, rewards, and money." – **Larry Hite**

"My philosophy is that all stocks are bad. There are no good stocks unless they go up in price. If they go down instead, you have to cut your losses fast...Letting losses run is the most serious mistake made by most investors." – **William O'Neil**

"When I became a winner, I said, 'I figured it out, but if I'm wrong, I'm getting the hell out, because I want to save my money and go on to the next trade.'" – **Marty Schwartz**

"Learn to take losses. The most important thing in making money is not letting your losses get out of hand." – **Marty Schwartz**

"I realised that this chipping away approach was what I should be doing, not putting myself at a big risk, trying to collect a ton of dough." – **Tony Saliba**

"When I get hurt in the market, I get the hell out. It doesn't matter at all where the market is trading. I just get out, because I believe that once you're hurt in the market, your decisions are going to be far less objective than they are when you're doing well...If you stick around when the market is severely against you, sooner or later they are going to carry you out." – **Randy McKay**

"I'll keep reducing my trading size as long as I'm losing...My money management techniques are extremely conservative. I never risk anything approaching the total amount of money in my account, let alone my total funds." – **Randy McKay**

"The elements of good trading are: (1) cutting losses, (2) cutting losses, and (3) cutting losses. If you can follow these three rules, you may have a chance." – **Ed Seykota**

"I always define my risk, and I don't have to worry about it." – **Tony Saliba**

Ignore money management and you will perish.

Part III

CHARTING

"Obviously the thing to do was to be bullish in a bull market
and bearish in a bear market. Sounds silly, doesn't it?"

Edwin Lefevre (Jesse Livermore),
Reminiscences of a Stock Operator, *1965*

7 TOOLS OF THE TRADE

I AM BY NATURE AND TRAINING a chartist or, if you prefer, a technical analyst. It is my belief that price action will tell you everything you need to know about a stock, an index or a currency. I have no faith whatsoever in fundamental analysis for a variety of reasons, but most of all, because it does not take into account the underlying psychology of the market. *People* make and move markets, not balance sheets.

The Role of Indicators

Many people confuse the generation of indicators and playing with technical analysis software as trading. It is not. I doubt you could find a truly proficient trader anywhere in the world who had much of an interest in indicators, let alone tell you what the pagan weighted ADX was.

If you spend all your time playing with indicators you are not a trader you are a hobbyist. There is no magic system. There is no Holy Grail. There is only discipline and common sense.

I have a series of core beliefs regarding indicators, and these include the following:

1. The more complicated they are the less likely they are to work. Just paid $15,000 for the Magic Super Secret Know-All Indicator course? I think the expression we are looking for is 'sucked in'. Simple systems and simple ideas work best. Markets can only do one of three things; go up, go down, go nowhere.

2. The more you know about your software probably the less you know about trading and the less trading you do. This is a direct inverse correlation; if you collect software and indicators chances are you don't spend much time working on the essentials of trading. If you don't spend any time on the essentials you won't make any money.

3. There is nothing new in indicators. They all seem to be either trend-following or oscillators. Likewise there is nothing new in markets.

4. There is a school of thought that says if I have one indicator then 25 should be 25 times better. This is a false assumption since it is based on the premise that it is the indicators that make the trader. In the real world it is the trader that makes the indicator. A good trader can make any system or tool work.

5. Indicators are a placebo—all they do is give you the confidence to pull the trigger, then the hard work starts.

6. To gain confidence look at the way the market behaves. Watch it, see how it ebbs and flows. Ed Seykota talks about being in tune to the ebbs and flows of the market. He even suggests that what traders who are struggling to find a rhythm should do is go down to the beach and stand in the water up to their thighs, shut their eyes and simply feel the water lap over them. When you are in tune with the water you will be able to anticipate the tempo of the ocean.

7. Don't worry about the indicators that I use, or that anyone else uses. What I do is irrelevant to you. It is rather like the assumption I made when I learned to play tennis in the 1970s. I imagined that if I used exactly the same tennis racket as Bjorn Borg then I would have to be unbeatable. Guess again.

8. If everyone else is using it and everyone else is losing money then what do you think the logical course of action is?

Information

Markets are merely a loose collection of individuals who seek consensus on price. As such, it is the psychology of these individuals that dictates where the market goes. A retort to this might be that investors read fundamental reports and then act on them. Unfortunately this is a naive assumption for two reasons.

Firstly, individuals act as filters for all the information they receive; each fact is measured against a set of personal, social and cultural biases and then incorporated into an individual's consciousness. Everything we do is coloured by our perceptions and expectations. Information is distorted and if it doesn't fit our beliefs it is discarded.

Such a phenomenon can be found in two disparate groups; pilots involved in crashes, and juries. It has been found that a growing number of aviation accidents are the result of pilot error. Many of these accidents occur because pilots' perceptions filter out and discard reality. An aircraft may be heading towards the ground yet if a pilot believes the plane is level then he will ignore his instrumentation with a rationalisation that it must be wrong. Similarly, juries are known to have made up their mind about a case generally by the end of the second day of a trial. What then happens is that they filter out any information that does not agree with their perceptions and concentrate only on that which agrees with their biases.

People who read, and more importantly produce, fundamental reports follow the same path. Their analysis is rarely objective as they are unwilling to shed their own bias. A cynical interpretation is that large broking houses derive a great deal of their revenue from corporate advisory work and institutional dealing. Brokers are therefore unwilling to bite the hand that feeds them. An additional point is that reports presented to shareholders by both companies and stockbroking firms are generally a thin concoction of exaggerations, half-truths and often bald-faced lies. Anyone who doubts this need only cast their mind back to glowing reports for companies such as Sausage Software, Davnet, Amazon.com and Priceline.

The second reason that fundamental analysis should be ignored is that markets often do not respond to new information. If fundamental analysis were correct then every small piece of information would cause the market to move in a given direction. Markets are perverse in that, depending on the mood of market participants, a piece of information may cause the market to do nothing, go up or go down. What happens is a reflection of the psychology of individual market participants, not the information.

What causes markets to change are perceptions, and the change of perceptions is a cultural phenomenon. I have lost count of the number of times I have seen a stock go up on bearish reports or go down on bullish reports.

I do have a further reason for not liking fundamental analysis. I have never met a fundamental analyst who has consistently made money out of the market. I have met analysts who get cocky during a bull run. Such analysts confuse skill with a roaring market. You just have to look at the quality of companies to list during such a buoyant phase in the market to realise that you could list your dog's kennel and it would attract buyers. All ships float on a rising tide.

My approach to charting is largely based on defining the underlying psychology of the market. As such there is a lot of emphasis on analysing the motives of traders as they are represented by various charts.

Magic Indicators

There is no magical technical indicator that will unlock the secrets of the market. This is a warning you will hear repeated often throughout this book. Many traders waste hundreds of hours searching for the one indicator that will tell the future; the one method of analysis that, if followed, will guarantee a vast fortune. No such indicator exists.

Of all the indicators available, and there are literally hundreds, I only use two or three on a regular basis. Various indicators have a variety of strengths and weaknesses. Some work exceptionally well in trending markets, some don't. Many will allow you to enter and exit the market at significant points such as tops and bottoms. Some will throw you around so badly in a directionless market that you will get whiplash. The point I am trying to make is that indicators come as a package. You must use a combination of techniques, so that the strengths and weaknesses of each are averaged out. You also need to consider your own psychology when selecting indicators. No indicator will overcome the person you are. There has not been an indicator invented that will negate the weakness of humans once they begin to use it.

Pattern Recognition

Don Quixote had the intriguing life ambition of being a knight. The only problem was that he mistook the windmills that dotted the Spanish countryside for dragons. This problem also besets traders who look for patterns in price action.

The first point of contact any trader has with the market is price action. Prices move in certain definable ways and each chart is a record of not only where the price action has occurred, but also the underlying psychology of the traders who make up any given market. When we view a chart we are given an insight into how traders are thinking. We can gauge their commitment to a trend, ascertain whether they are anxious or excited. Most importantly we can use these insights to aid making our own trading more profitable.

> *"If a pattern is not immediately recognisable, it simply does not exist."*

Charts display reproducible patterns. These formations occur time and time again in markets as diverse as stocks, commodities and the various inter-bank markets. There is nothing mysterious about this fact. Such mundane repetition is to be expected since all markets are made up of individuals, each of whom is buffeted by the contrary emotions of fear and greed. It is only logical to expect these patterns to reproduce themselves as traders reproduce the actions of the traders who went before them.

A raw chart of price action is probably the most powerful tool that we have as traders. What we are seeing is pure price action and by extension the actions and motivations of traders. Such raw analysis is unencumbered by complex analytical methods that have the capacity to filter and inadvertently distort information. Traders should get to know how various markets perform on a daily basis. By doing so they will raise their level of intuition regarding whichever commodity they are trading.

Interpreting Price Data

In examining how to interpret price data in the following chapters I will only touch on what I consider to be the most powerful and effective patterns. I do this for several reasons. These patterns are clearly defined and easy to recognise: as such they are not prone to subjectivity. The less we allow subjective interpretation the less room for error we have in our trading method.

Significant Reference Points

Much of the way I trade is based upon understanding the psychology and motivations of other traders and how these factors manifest themselves in the market. The psychology of traders is displayed in the patterns of price movement that show up on simple charts. The points we are most interested in are referred to as 'significant reference points'. This term was first used by Mark Douglas in his excellent book, *The Disciplined Trader*. Douglas defines a significant reference point as anything that causes traders' expectations to be raised about the possibility of something happening. They are the points where a large number of traders have taken opposing positions. Based upon those expectations, they will continue to hold a position in the belief that the expectation will be fulfilled and, most important, they will likely liquidate a position as a result of the expectation being unfulfilled.

The relevance of those areas to traders can be further examined by using derivative markets as an example. Since derivatives, such as futures, allow traders to be both long and short the market, it is easy to conceive of futures prices moving rapidly up and down.

Let's assume that I am long the Share Price Index (SPI) futures contract at 3100. In taking this position my expectation is that the Index will go up from this point. In order for me to take this position a trader with a contrary point of view has to sell me a contract. By definition, his point of view is that the market will go down.

As part of this example let us also assume that the SPI has been trading at 3100 for a few days. As the contract trades at this level, traders with opposing points of view are taking a stand based upon what they have prescribed as the way the market should behave. Consequently we have a zone of churning. If the market breaks up from this level then it reinforces the significance of 3100 in the minds of both buyers and sellers. The buyers remember 3100 as a point from which they were profitable and their point of view was validated. Whereas the sellers remember it as a level from which the market moved away from them, leaving their perceptions unfulfilled.

If a great number of sellers all held the same view then we have a large population of traders who have to reverse their opinions and begin to compete with the buyers for whatever positions remain available. The importance of this becomes obvious if the SPI begins to track back to 3100. As it does so traders who were short the index at this point are unwilling to short the index again, since it was from here that the market reversed on them. Those who had been long the SPI recognise it as a level from which they were profitable. Each side has once again decided in advance what course of action the market should take. The more traders who were involved in the initial move the more significance the position will have in the future.

If we can understand part of what traders are thinking when prices behave in certain ways then we have gone a long way to increasing the profitability of our trading. Whilst the term 'significant reference points' may seem a little grandiose, it is appropriate in that it highlights that each time traders make a decision at a certain price then this price is significant for them. Therefore they will behave in a certain manner that we as traders are able to interpret. Any chart pattern you see is just a variation on this theme of buyers and sellers with competing perceptions.

8 | GAPS

OFTEN WHEN YOU VIEW a chart you will see holes in the price action. These holes denote gaps or days when prices have moved away from the previous day's close. For example, a gap in the All Ordinaries Index would occur if on Wednesday the Index closed at its high of 3200 and on Thursday it opened at 3175, and during the course of Thursday trading it did not trade back towards Wednesday's close.

Gaps often occur when powerful news from another market hits our market overnight. In such a situation traders queue their orders up before trading begins, pushing prices beyond the ranges experienced the day before.

A gap represents a significant change in the mood of traders. This change may have been due to the release of a certain news item that has caught the market unaware, a significant move in another market, or it may simply result from an acceleration of an existing trend. This acceleration may be exacerbated because of the way the Stock Exchange Automated Trading System (SEATS) dealing system averages prices on open. As a result of this the gap you see may simply be an artefact, a result of the technology we use to transact business. Whilst I have no definitive evidence for it I can speculate that markets were more prone to gapping in the late 1990s than they were in prior years.

Whether the gap results from a true change in the environment surrounding a stock or is simply a function of the new dealing regime and greater amateur participation in the market is irrelevant. What is important is how you trade these punctuations in price.

Trading Gaps

In formulating rules for trading these events it is necessary to distinguish between the three major types of gaps. These are breakaway gaps, continuation gaps and exhaustion gaps.

Breakaway Gaps

These are sudden breaks in price, and they represent the most significant change in market sentiment. They are generally accompanied by an increase in volume. For a downward gap, this increase in volume is the result of two diametrically opposed views. The first—and in my opinion correct—view is that sentiment has changed and any long positions should be exited, and if possible new short positions initiated. The contrary view—and in my opinion the incorrect one—is that the drop in price represents an opportunity to purchase more stock.

> *"These are sudden breaks in price...and they represent the most significant change in market sentiment."*

The first view is the correct one for trend-followers. The second view is incorrect for trend-followers since they are trading contrary to the trend. The second view is also incorrect from a trading point of view. As I have said many times, never buy anything that is going down.

FIGURE 8.1   DAVNET BREAKAWAY GAP

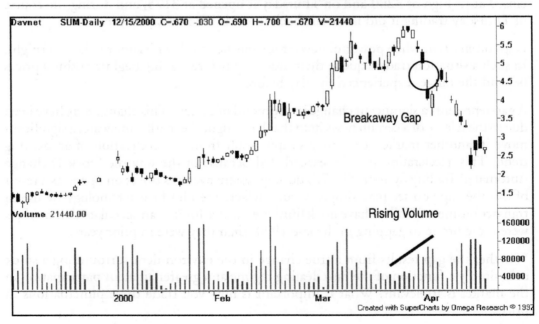

90

In this example volume accelerates as the gap opens up. This is the smart money exiting the position. This smart money continues to sell into the decline and open up new short positions. The bulls are quickly swamped and a downtrend is initiated.

The trading of breakaway or initial gaps is considered to be a very aggressive strategy, but is it really? The market is showing you which way it wants to go. Why is going in the direction of the market considered to be aggressive when it should be considered to be a very commonsense approach?

Gaps also allow traders to find a logical place to put their initial stops. In Figure 8.1 the stock made a double top at approximately $6.00. It then gapped down on a lift in volume. Therefore it would only be logical to place a stop for any short sale position at this $6.00 point since this could be considered the point of maximum adverse excursion.

A short sale trade in DVT based upon the appearance of a gap at this point would take on the following appearance:

Trading float = $50,000

2% risk premium = $1,000

Entry price = $5.40

Stop loss = $6.00

Position size = $6.00 – $5.40 = 60¢

$1,000/60¢ = 1,666 shares that can be short sold @ $5.40, giving $8,996.40 exposure to the stock

Note that given this is a short sale position the trader need only put up approximately a 20% margin, or about $1,800.

This breakaway gap provides a valuable trading signal and an ideal place from which to launch an assault on the stock.

Continuation Gaps

Breakaway gaps herald a change in sentiment. Continuation gaps confirm that this trend is still in place. Referring to DVT again (see Figure 8.2, overleaf) it can be seen that after the initial explosion downwards, the move continued.

FIGURE 8.2 DAVNET GAPS

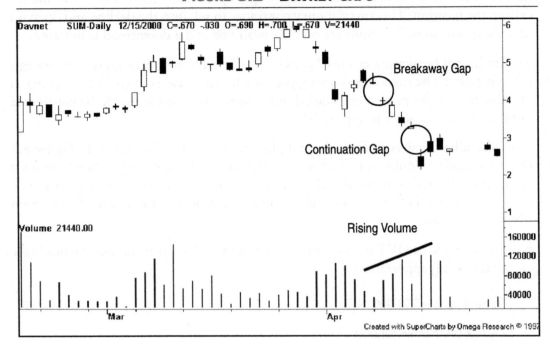

Continuation gaps allow those traders who require more confirmation to engage the stock whilst the move is still under way. In this example the continuation gaps would have allowed a trader to either pyramid into the existing short sale position or initiate a new position if the initial move had been missed.

Continuation gaps are also confirmed by an increase in volume, as the smart money continues to sell the stock and amateur bulls try to bottom-fish. During this phase of price action the bears are in charge and the bulls, whilst trying to hold the line, are simply being swamped by the sellers. The sellers may not be actively seeking to short the stock. One of the great myths of trading is that when price moves against a bullish position it must be because of the evil short sellers. A more plausible explanation is that anyone who is bullish during a bearish move is simply wrong, just as anyone who is bearish during a bullish phase is wrong.

I must stress breakaway and continuation gaps are not confined to down moves. Under the right circumstances it is just as easy for a stock to gap upwards. In the following example (Figure 8.3, opposite) Biota (BTA) has three bullish gaps that push prices higher.

FIGURE 8.3 BIOTA BULLISH GAPS

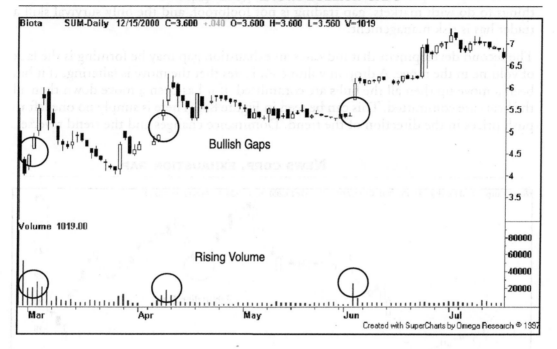

Exhaustion gaps act as traps for those who are not able to distinguish them from their counterparts. This difficulty is heightened by the fact that exhaustion gaps often have all the hallmarks of continuation gaps.

Exhaustion Gaps

Exhaustion gaps are also known as sucker gaps. They occur in the terminal phase of a move. The exhaustion gap is a dangerous beast for the unwary. Exhaustion gaps often occur in the last leg of a move and represent a last ditch effort by the dominant group to drive prices in their preferred direction. However it should not be construed that this is an active decision made by the group as a whole. It is merely the market's usual process of risk and wealth transference in action.

The terminal phases of moves are populated by novice traders acting under either a lack of knowledge or poor advice. Exhaustion gaps act as traps for those who are not able to distinguish them from their counterparts. This difficulty is heightened by the fact that exhaustion gaps often have all the hallmarks of continuation gaps.

The first clue to the formation of an exhaustion gap is that prices do not continue in the direction of the trend. In both a breakaway and continuation gap prices move in the direction of the trend and the gap is not filled in for a considerable period of time. In an exhaustion gap prices begin to slip back into the hole created by the gap. This is the first sign that the market is losing momentum and any trade in the direction of the trend must be closed in anticipation of a reversal. This is why it is wise to have a

93

defined stop loss point in mind when entering into gap-initiated trades. As with all things to do with markets, gap trading is not foolproof, and the only survival skill a trader has is risk management.

The second development that indicates an exhaustion gap may be forming is the lack of volume in the move. A drop in volume indicates that the move is faltering. If it has been a move up then all the bulls are committed, if it has been a move down then all the bears are committed. This can be seen in Figure 8.4. There is simply no one left to push prices in the direction of the trend. Dominance changes and the trend reverses.

FIGURE 8.4   NEWS CORP. EXHAUSTION GAP

False Gaps

False gaps are traditionally caused by two events. Firstly a share going ex-dividend will cause the share price to adjust. These gaps are obvious, and all traders should be aware of the timing of dividends. The second reason for false gaps is difficulties with data. The majority of data used by Australian traders is of poor quality. As a result their databases are full of what are known as bad ticks. These may result from missing days or an incorrect adjustment of a share split. This is also problematic in futures data, where back-data may not have been correctly adjusted for continuous contracts thereby giving the impression of a gap in the trend.

9   TRIANGLES

TRIANGLES ARE AREAS OF CONGESTION where bulls and bears fight for ascendancy. A triangle may either serve as a continuation pattern or a reversal pattern. This is most often the case with small triangles of which the height is between 10% and 15% of the range of the preceeding trend. Such triangles merely serve to interrupt the current trend but they do not displace the prevailing sentiment. An example of a small triangle that serves as a continuation pattern may be seen in the following chart of HIH.

FIGURE 9.1   HIH TRIANGLE CONTINUATION PATTERN

This triangle is merely a punctuation in the overall downtrend that characterised the market activity in HIH. Its place in the overall scheme of price action can be seen in the more expanded chart (Figure 9.2, below). This interruption gives the bulls false hope, and they re-enter the market in the expectation of a reversal pattern developing. In this instance the triangle acts as a bull trap.

FIGURE 9.2   HIH LONG TERM

HIH Ins   SUM-Daily 10/20/2000 C=.425 +.005 O=.425 H=.435 L=.420 V=12506

Created with SuperCharts by Omega Research © 1997

> **"Triangles that are large relative to the predominant trend will reverse the prevailing trend..."**

Triangles may also act as reversal patterns. Triangles that are large relative to the predominant trend will reverse the prevailing trend, and are indicative of a pivot shift in the prevailing psychology of the market. The chart of Macquarie Infrastructure Group (MIG—Figure 9.3, opposite) shows a large triangular break from congestion into an uptrend formation.

The classification of triangles into large and small is somewhat simplistic. A better gauge of market action is to classify triangles into their three types; symmetrical, ascending and descending.

FIGURE 9.3 MIG BREAKOUT

Symmetrical Triangles

In a symmetrical triangle the upper and lower boundaries of the triangle have an equal angle of incidence. In simple terms the upper and lower boundaries look the same, as can be seen in the example of National Bank (NAB—below).

FIGURE 9.4 NAB SYMMETRICAL TRIANGLE

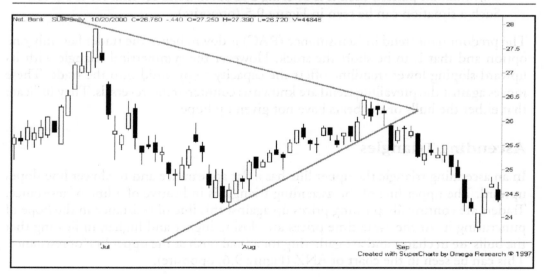

Symmetrical triangles are of little predictive value since they indicate an equilibrium between the bulls and the bears. As such they are most likely to simply be a continuation pattern. They are nice to draw but offer little predictive value. If a symmetrical triangle occurs within an uptrend then it is likely to be a continuation pattern for that uptrend. If it occurs within a downtrend then it is likely to be a continuation pattern for the downtrend.

Trading Rules for Symmetrical Triangles

1. Firstly, a survival rule; if you are inexperienced do not try and trade inside the body of the triangle since you may be trading false breaks which can quickly reverse.

2. Try to determine if the triangle is likely to break to the upside or the downside. This can be done by converting the chart to a weekly chart. If the weekly trend is up then it is likely to break to the upside. If the weekly trend is down it is likely to break to the downside. It is rare in my experience for symmetrical triangles to be reversal patterns.

3. For placing trades it is necessary to have a confirmation signal such as a break through the upper or lower boundary of the triangle. If going long then a buy stop can be placed above the upper boundary. If going short then place the sell order below the lower boundary. It may be necessary to confirm the move by placing the orders one or two ticks beyond the breakout price.

4. The movement inside a symmetrical triangle may provide the experienced trader with an opportunity to pyramid into an existing trade. If the triangle is a continuation pattern then it is offering a counter-trend reversal for the trader. Such a situation can be seen in Figure 9.5 (opposite).

The predominant trend in Reinsurance (RAC) is down, hence the trader has only one option and that is to be short the stock. However the symmetrical triangle with its upward-sloping lower trendline offers the capacity to pyramid into the trade. These moves against the prevailing trend are known as counter-trend reversals. They indicate that either the bulls or the bears have not given up hope.

Ascending Triangles

In an ascending triangle the upper line has a flat appearance and the lower line slopes upward. The upper line of the ascending triangle is indicative of a line of resistance. Traders are continually pushing prices up against this line of resistance in the hope of puncturing it. At the same time prices are closing higher and higher, indicating that the bulls are in charge and are gathering for a final push at the upper line of resistance. This can be seen in the chart of ANZ (Figure 9.6, opposite).

FIGURE 9.5 REINSURANCE SYMMETRICAL TRIANGLE

FIGURE 9.6 ANZ ASCENDING TRIANGLE

It is necessary to build into the trading of ascending triangles a methodology to enter the trade. The formation of the triangle is only a set-up, it is not the trigger. The trigger is the break out of the triangular formation.

If the ANZ breakout is examined more closely rules can be generated for the trade initiation.

Trading Rules for Ascending Triangles

1. A line of resistance is a point where the bears have a temporary dominance.

2. In this instance there is a clean break of the line of support by a trigger day. This initial trigger is often followed by a fall back towards the line of resistance, which has now become a support.

3. To overcome being caught in a re-test of the line of support a conditional trigger needs to be introduced. This may be a lift in volume (see Figure 9.7, opposite) or it can be a secondary trigger such as a move of 1ATR beyond the line of support or two higher highs after the breakout.

> *"The formation of the triangle is only a set-up, it is not the trigger. The trigger is the break out of the triangular formation."*

An interesting thing happens in this particular trade. The break through fails completely and the price collapses back into a congestion zone below the initial level of support (see Figure 9.8, opposite). I have two theories as to why this happened. Firstly the initial ascending triangle was quite mature and as such both bulls and bears were fatigued from an extended struggle. Secondly the breakout occurred in a very uncertain market. At the time of writing market dynamics have changed substantially and false breakouts appear to be the norm.

Descending Triangles

Descending triangles have a flat base and a downward-sloping upper trendline. They are the reverse of the ascending triangle as the lower trendline acts as support and the downward-sloping upper boundary indicates that traders are closing the market at lower and lower prices. The bears are gathering strength for a push through the lower trendline.

In descending triangles prices traditionally break to the downside. Hence the triangle is a set-up. It alerts the trader to the possibility of a sharp break in market sentiment. The trigger to enter a trade is a sustained move through the line of resistance.

FIGURE 9.7 **ANZ** TRIGGER

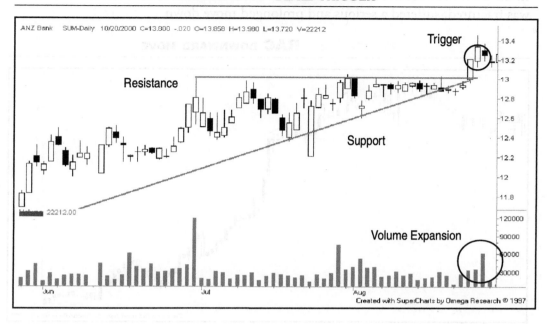

FIGURE 9.8 **ANZ** DROP IN PRICE

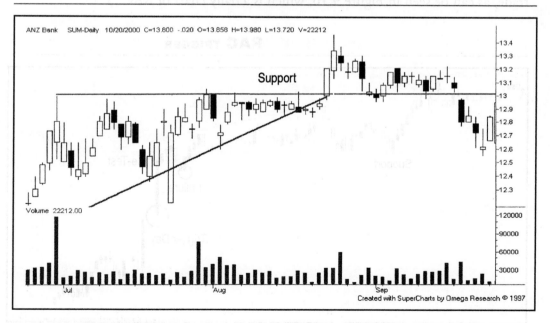

In the chart below I have shown a weekly chart of RAC which, once the lower trendline was fractured, suffered a serious and prolonged move down.

FIGURE 9.9   **RAC** DOWNWARD MOVE

However this chart is only a set-up, and as such a trader still needs a trigger to enter the trade, as can be seen in Figure 9.10, which is a daily chart of RAC.

FIGURE 9.10   **RAC** TRIGGER

Trading Rules for Descending Triangles

1. There is a clearly defined line of support. This is where the bulls have drawn a line in the sand, and if price moves beyond this then they will join the selling.

2. An initial failure of the line of support is usually characterised by a lack of volume in the down move. This can be considered to be a probing move by the bears.

3. A re-test of the line of support on diminished volume means that the bulls have lost momentum and cannot move prices beyond the line of resistance.

4. A trigger day is a sustained powerful move under increasing volume. This is the day on which traders should look to enter a position. If traders need additional confirmation of a move down they may want to build a conditional statement into their trigger. This condition may be something along the lines of: enter in direction of the breakdown if the move is 1ATR away from the line of resistance.

Predictive Value

Much is made of the predictive value of the triangle in terms of the dimension of the move out of the triangle. The conventional wisdom is that if you measure the width of the triangle at its base you can use this as a guide to how far price will move when price breaks out of the triangle. I must admit I have seen only a limited validity of this concept.

The predictive value of the triangle is in suggesting the direction of the breakout, not its duration. Ascending and descending triangles are merely an extension of the concept of support and resistance. It is these two concepts that are pivotal to the successful trading of triangles. The predictive value of a triangle is lessened as the triangle matures. If a triangle breaks through at the apex, as was the case with ANZ, then the move is likely to stagnate. Ideally a move should accelerate into the triangle and then burst out as sentiment changes.

Congestion

I want to briefly review congestion (also referred to as consolidation) in terms of trying to generate some simple trading rules. It is important that traders become familiar with consolidating since this is what price spends most of its time doing. It is also from congestion that explosive moves are made. Stan Weinstein in his excellent book *Secrets for Profiting from Bull and Bear Markets* (Irwin Financial Press, 1988) characterises periods of base consolidation as being stage one in the life-cycle of price movements.

Traditionally congestion is presented as being fairly clean, with all the peaks and troughs being very similar. This is the impression that could be gathered from viewing the chart of Pacific Dunlop (PDP—below).

FIGURE 9.11 PACIFIC DUNLOP CONSOLIDATION

However, congestion zones are very bumpy, almost chaotic environments. A better idea of how dynamic these areas can be is seen when the area is expanded (below).

FIGURE 9.12 PACIFIC DUNLOP CONSOLIDATION EXPANDED

As can be seen prices do not move perfectly between two extremes—they often stall and form secondary zones of congestion. I feel it is necessary to put congestion into place because many novice traders look at congestion zones and think: well all I have to do is buy at the low and sell at the high. As such they often try and trade ranges, with disastrous consequences. Ranges sap confidence and chew up capital. Traders profit by trading the break out of the zone, so they must know how to recognise such zones. This is—as with most things—very easy in hindsight. The application of some simple rules may help.

Trading Rules for Congestion Zones

1. Plot the zone of congestion. This can be done manually or with the assistance of an indicator. True swings should be plotted from high to low as these mark extremes in market psychology.

2. Determine the highest peak or swing in the congestion zone. This becomes the reference point for the breakout.

3. The congestion is a set-up. The breakout is determined by a breach of the peak of the last major pivot. In the chart of Sausage (overleaf) the major pivot is the first pivot in the congestion zone.

4. Determine a trigger for entry into a position. The trigger may be a breach of the major pivot high plus two successively higher closes. If the trader is more aggressive this may be a single close above the pivot, or it may be a breach of the major pivot plus 1ATR.

Zones of congestion must be plotted. This can be done by using a simple indicator known as ZIG ZAG (see Figure 9.13, overleaf), which is available in both Metastock and SuperCharts. The use of a mechanical technique removes much of the subjective interpretation inherent in technical analysis. It also provides a basis for the building of trading rules.

As can be seen the application of the ZIG ZAG indicator places a series of peak-to-trough lines through the price. In doing so it highlights the congestion zone. Before proceeding it should be noted that this indicator in Metastock is imperfect in that it only allows the placement of swings from either the close to close, high to high, open to open or low to low. It will also redraw the swings as new data is added, whereas SuperCharts has the capacity to build in a strength value so that the swing is only engaged after passing certain criteria.

FIGURE 9.13   SAUSAGE WITH ZIG ZAG INDICATOR

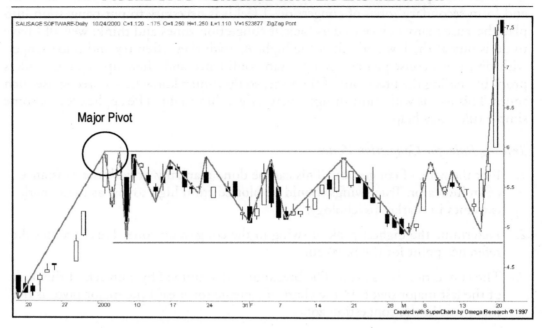

TOPS AND BOTTOMS

The Double Top

The double top is an obvious trading signal. It is formed as a result of a faltering in a sustained uptrend. As this uptrend reaches its apex a point is arrived at where the demand created by all the buyers is met and the momentum of the move begins to decay. At this point there is a subtle switch in the dynamics of the market and price begins to slip backwards. This slippage may be due to either natural profit-taking —it may be felt that beyond a certain price valuations for a stock become a little extreme—or it could simply be part of the cycle that price evolves through.

Whatever the reason for the intervention by sellers this high point becomes an area of significance to both those who are long the market and those who have entered the market on the short side. Both sides of the market now have an emotional stake in this price region; the bulls because a move beyond this point validates their long positions, the bears because a fall away from this point validates their decision to either exit the stock or trade the short side.

As a double top unfolds there is a transient move down in price. This move downwards, whilst only temporary in nature, can cause substantial slippage in price as the momentum swings temporarily towards the bears. Low prices rally as the bulls reassert themselves. It is worth noting that in a double top the underlying broad uptrend may not suffer that much slippage, so traders have to be both perceptive and light on their feet to catch the top as it forms.

As the bulls re-enter the market price moves back towards the previous high. It is here that the earlier discussion on significant reference points is revisited. The descent from the previous high was where those who were short the market were able to make a profit, whereas those who were long the market suffered the pain of being on the wrong side of the market, hence the previous high is firmly entrenched in the minds of all market participants. I must admit that this is a generalisation because the majority of traders have no idea why they behave in the way they do.

As the market rallies back to its previous high, sellers begin to enter the market, catching the last of the bulls by surprise. After all the available demand is met, the sellers then begin to drive the market down. Realising their error those who were long now have to compete with the sellers and offer their stock at lower and lower prices in order to attract buyers.

As price begins to slip the standard mechanism of competition among traders is engaged. They begin to outbid one another on the downside in order to exit the position. Only those who are most aggressive win so prices are pushed down, often with remarkable speed.

FIGURE 10.1 TELSTRA DOUBLE TOP

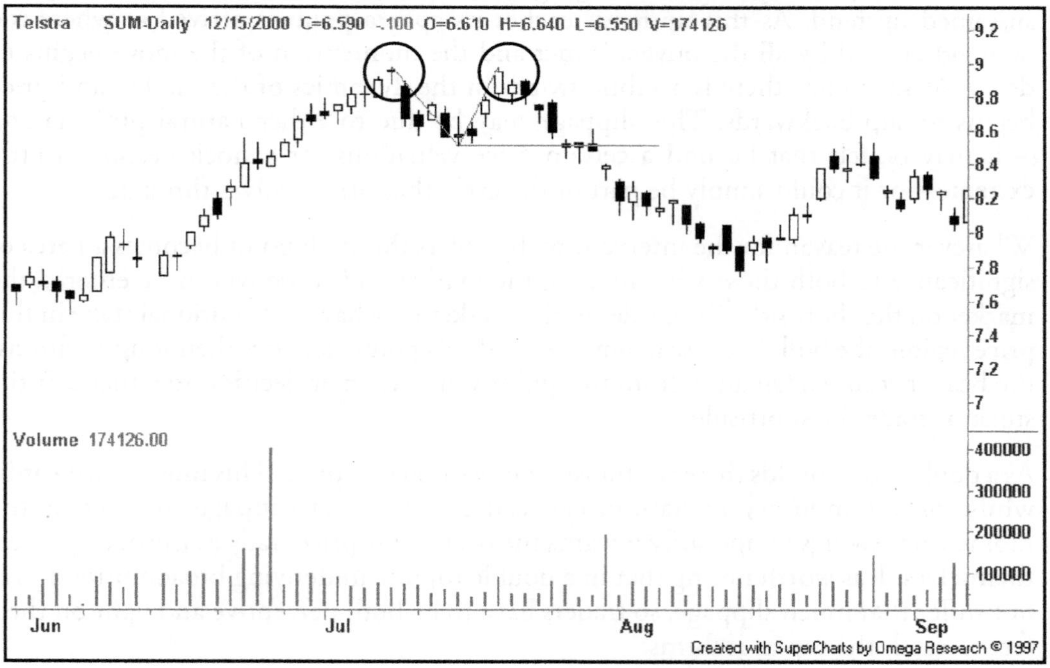
Telstra SUM-Daily 12/15/2000 C=6.590 -.100 O=6.610 H=6.640 L=6.550 V=174126
9.2
9
8.8
8.6
8.4
8.2
8
7.8
7.6
7.4
7.2
7
Volume 174126.00
400000
300000
200000
100000
Jun
Jul
Aug
Sep
Created with SuperCharts by Omega Research © 1997

In Figure 10.1 I have highlighted the two peaks. Between the two peaks is the first retracement. To the right of this the trendline represents the lowest point of the retracement. In analysing double tops much is made of this low point; the argument goes along the lines of it is not a double top unless this low is taken out on the downside. There is some merit to this argument since confirmation does provide an element of apparent safety. The counter argument is that a line of resistance has been formed and that trades can be launched from this resistance.

The answer to this conundrum is that there is no answer; there is no perfectly safe way to engage a trade. They all carry risk, even something as obvious as a double top. In trading the only indication you need is something that eases your doubts sufficiently to pull the trigger. If you are capable of pulling the trigger the instant the reversal from a double top occurs then trade accordingly. If you require further confirmation then wait. No one way is better than the next.

In examining these types of formations there is also some debate as to whether you go on double tops that have been formed by extremes of sentiment during the day or whether you go on double tops formed by closing prices. Once again it does not matter—both provide a signal to trade, as can be seen in the below chart of Telstra's closing prices for the same period.

FIGURE 10.2 TELSTRA DOUBLE TOP ON CLOSING PRICES

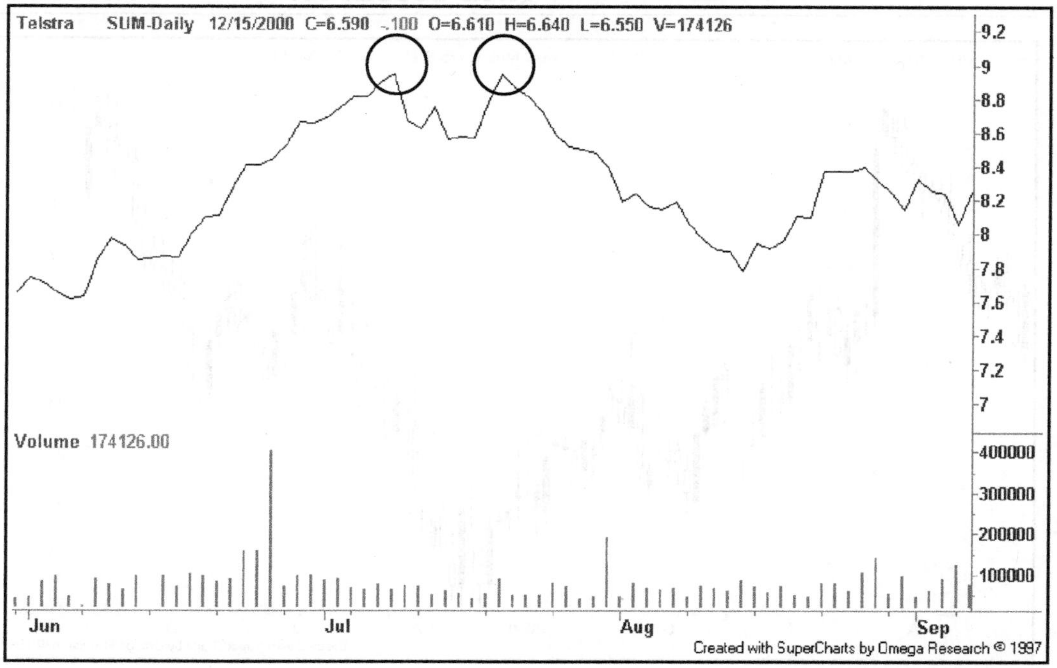

Time Scales

I consider the time scale over which such formations occur to be somewhat irrelevant. Double tops can occur several days, several weeks or several months apart. The only stipulation I place on this is that tops occurring on sequential days lack much directional energy except in the case of what are known as outside days. Candle enthusiasts call them tweezer tops. In this situation the range of trading of the second day engulfs the first day and the close is lower.

> *"Double tops are merely extended zones of resistance. There is nothing special or mystical about them..."*

Double tops are merely extended zones of resistance. There is nothing special or mystical about them, they are merely a subset of all resistance formations. As can be seen they occur in all timeframes. In fact they may force traders to look at the bigger picture and to consider what they are seeing in the wider context of the price history of a given instrument.

To illustrate the possible time scales over which double tops can occur consider the following three examples.

FIGURE 10.3   NAB DOUBLE TOP

FIGURE 10.4 TELSTRA DOUBLE TOP

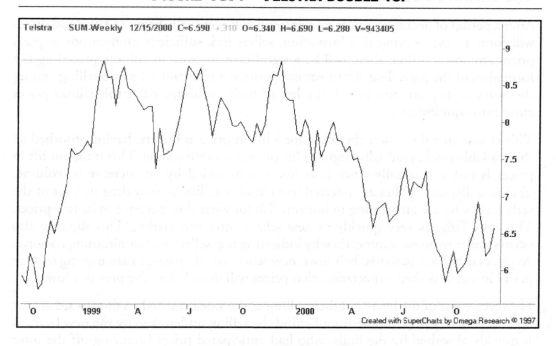

FIGURE 10.5 AGL DOUBLE TOP

The Double Bottom

After a period of declining prices a downtrend will eventually begin to falter and prices will form a base. During this formation, sellers lack sufficient momentum to push prices any lower. Often there will be a significant increase in volume preceding the formation of the base. This lift in volume is often a reflection of panic-selling among the bears as they attempt to exit the last of their positions. After this climax prices enter into equilibrium.

This climax in volume sets the scene for a lift in price as buyers, having absorbed all the available stock, gradually begin to lift prices on inertia alone. This transient lift in prices is not a true rally since it is not accompanied by an increase in volume. Traditionally, such rallies are referred to as 'sucker rallies' as they drag in a lot of the stale bulls who are attempting to bottom-fish for what they perceive to be low prices. This rally fatigues very quickly as new sellers enter the market. This slippage also occurs under reduced volume, thereby indicating that sellers are a diminishing resource. As prices drift back towards their lows, new sellers are often caught attempting to push prices lower. It is their expectation that prices will drop below the previous low.

However, most of the bears did their selling as the stock reached its downward climax and there is very little momentum behind the selling undertaken by the new bears. It is quickly absorbed by the bulls, who had anticipated prices bouncing off the most recent low. The bulls gradually begin to bid prices up. Those sellers who had only recently taken positions are caught on the wrong side of the market and have to compete with the bulls for whatever positions are available. Gradually the ascendancy shifts and prices explode out of their lows.

Occasionally this leg will falter and two scenarios are possible; prices fall through the last low as sellers regain their momentum and swamp the available buyers, or the low holds and a triple bottom is formed thereby generating a further bullish signal.

As can be seen in the example of Davnet (Figure 10.6, opposite) there is panic-selling as the stock approaches the interim low of approximately $1.00. Volume then contracts. It then accelerates again as price re-tests this level, only to bounce off.

As can be seen the double bottom is merely the inverse of a double top—the same psychology applies but in reverse. Just as in a double top it may have been notions of how expensive a stock may have become that prompted the weakness, in the case of a double bottom it may be notions of how cheap a stock has become or what sort of bargain it may represent at a certain price. These considerations are largely irrelevant. What is important is that the price action created by these perceptions generates a tradeable signal.

FIGURE 10.6   DAVNET DOUBLE BOTTOM

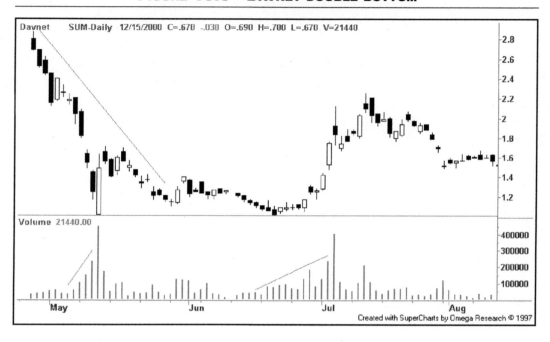

Conclusion

Do not become too precious about your interpretation of patterns within the stock market. Pick up most texts relating to pattern recognition and you will see an infinite variety of almost perfect patterns each drawn with a loving clarity. Unfortunately for us the real world does not work this way. Our signals need to be flexible. Do not have a nervous breakdown if price does not form perfectly aligned peaks or troughs—merely take the signal and make the trade. If you have proper risk management there is very little that can go wrong.

11 TRENDS

TRENDS ARE THE cornerstone of trading. It is impossible to trade against the trend. This may seem obvious in the extreme yet it is paradoxically so obvious that the majority of investors miss the point. If the market is going up, you go long; if the market is going down, you go short. Before I look at why this is seemingly so difficult it is necessary to consider a few of the basics of trend types.

Up, Down and Sideways

An uptrend is defined as a series of higher highs and higher lows. A downtrend is defined as a series of lower highs and lower lows. Consider the following example of the CRB futures contract during part of its trading history (Figure 11.1, overleaf).

Clearly it can be seen that as prices swing upward there is a series of higher highs, and the lows experienced by the instrument also rise. Conversely, a downtrend is characterised by a series of lower highs and deepening lows.

Uptrends occur because there are not enough sellers present in the marketplace to absorb all the buyers who are competing with one another. As buyers compete, the number of sellers diminishes, forcing buyers to offer higher and higher prices in order to gain a place in the market. This upward dynamic is enhanced by the presence of old sellers who exited the market at lower levels and are now trying to re-enter the market, thereby further adding to the competition between buyers.

FIGURE 11.1 **CRB** FUTURES UPTREND

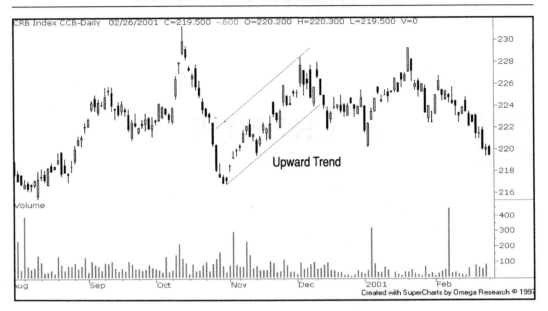

Downtrends are generated when the available sellers swamp the resources of the buyers in the market. Sellers are then forced to compete with one another in order to exit the market. This competition takes the form of lower and lower prices. Eventually this downward momentum is sufficient to drive prices down in a sustained trend. In markets that allow short selling this pressure is exacerbated by old buyers who, perceiving an opportunity to trade, join the sellers and add to the level of competition.

Markets do not always go up or down. Much of the time any given instrument may simply move sideways in a well-defined pattern. Such a trend is not surprisingly called a sideways trend. These markets present a unique challenge to traders, and can be responsible for a significant decay in equity if traders are unaware that a market is drifting. There are specialised techniques for trading a sideways market, and I will touch on those shortly. As an example of a sideways trend consider the following example of NAB (Figure 11.2, opposite).

After a spectacular uptrend NAB settled into a sideways congestion pattern. Within such a pattern bulls and bears are fighting for dominance. Such patterns reveal a great deal of uncertainty inherent within the market participants. Generally sideways trends are a little like a pressure cooker; the longer they persist the more spectacular the breakout when they end. These sudden explosions of activity occur for the simple reason that each time a stock bounces off the upper or lower band of a trend, the views of a particular group of traders are confirmed.

116

FIGURE 11.2 **NAB** SIDEWAYS TREND

If we take the example of NAB, every time the stock touched $30 and then retreated all those who were short NAB either by short selling the stock or via options trades had their views confirmed. As such their confidence increased and they added to their positions or new sellers were enticed into the market. Eventually the sellers were unable to contain the bulls and the stock lifted out of its trench. As the stock lifted the bears who had been so confident were now faced with a losing position. They sought to cover their short positions by competing with the new buyers for the available stock, thus driving the price up. The astute reader will have realised that the same but opposite dynamic was occurring every time NAB touched the lower edge of the trend and that, had the overwhelming group sentiment been negative, then NAB could have broken down instead of lifting out of the trench.

Timeframes

As well as being broken down into three main categories, trends can also be broken down into three timeframes: long, intermediate and short term. Again such a remark may seem obvious but traders often have difficulty deciding what timeframe they are interested in. A portfolio trader may only be interested in long-term movements whereas a more active trader, such as an options trader, will be interested in daily movements.

If we view the following three charts of the All Ords we can see that there is an enormous variation in the formations shown on a chart merely by altering the time scale. For example, if I were a day trader it would be pointless for me to look at either the monthly or weekly chart except to view the market in its historical context. It would be impossible for me to trade the All Ords each day based upon a weekly or a monthly chart. Likewise if I were an options trader in BHP I would not rely on weekly or monthly charts.

However, if I were a portfolio trader and I was only interested in catching the large swings in the market then I would ignore daily price fluctuations in preference for weekly or monthly movements. Still, though, traders frequently make their decisions based on the wrong chart.

FIGURE 11.3   DAILY CHART

FIGURE 11.4   WEEKLY CHART

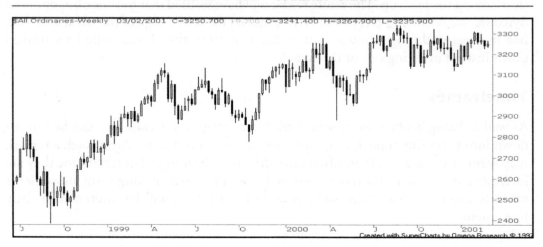

FIGURE 11.5 MONTHLY CHART

It is also important to note that, whilst a monthly chart may be trending up, the weekly chart may be trending down and the daily chart may be directionless.

Why do Trends Change?

As can be seen by any of our earlier charts several things are apparent about trends. Firstly, within each broad movement there are smaller perturbations or breaks in the underlying trend, which are only temporary in nature. Secondly, trends don't go on forever; they eventually break and reverse. Market participants who enter the market during a bull run seem to live under the misapprehension that the market only goes one way. There is no such thing as an elevator that only goes up.

Within each trend are what are called retracements. These retracements are small movements of the price against the underlying trend.

For example, in the chart of Amcor (see Figure 11.6, overleaf), as the stock rallies in a general upward direction throughout the year there are

> *"Market participants who enter the market during a bull run seem to live under the misapprehension that the market only goes one way."*

periods when it seems to falter and prices fall back without breaking the underlying upward trend. These small slippages are retracements. In an upward-trending market retracements occur because buyers who entered the market at lower levels are exiting the stock, thereby creating some downward momentum.

119

FIGURE 11.6 AMCOR RESISTANCE

A break in an uptrend will only occur when sellers arrive in sufficient numbers to overwhelm the available supply of buyers. As this happens sellers begin to compete with each other for the available buyers and as a result downward momentum is created and the stock begins to fall back. As the price of the stock deteriorates new buyers who have entered the stock at much higher levels panic and accelerate the level of competition among sellers, thus driving the price down and breaking the trend.

A reverse of an uptrend may be a temporary phenomenon or it may signify the arrival of a bear market. The chart opposite (Figure 11.7) displays the reverse of the trend in the Nasdaq in 2000.

Bear markets are substantial breaks in uptrends that may accompany cataclysmic events —like the crash of '87—or they may be prolonged downtrends. The reason why bull markets such as that experienced in the mid-'80s turn into bear markets by breaking their uptrend is because of the involvement of the general investing public. As a market runs up and amateur investors get involved, the tolerance for risk in the market changes. Amateur investors have the least tolerance for risk and as such need constant reassurance that they are doing the right thing and that their chosen course of action has a high degree of certainty to it. This reassurance may come from other amateurs, such as friends who are also involved in the market and therefore do not wish to confront the possibility of a break in trend, or it may come from semi-professionals like stockbrokers who also have a vested interest in the trend continuing.

FIGURE 11.7   NASDAQ BREAK IN TRENDS

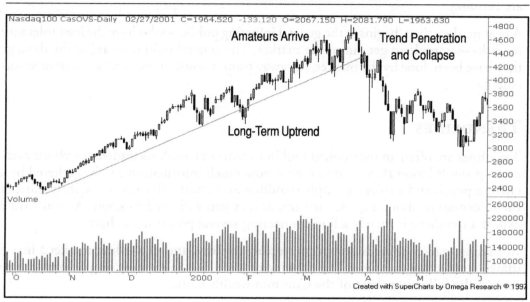

During the later stages of a strong uptrend most market participants have a very narrow comfort zone and they become very distressed once the market begins to move away from what they consider to be 'proper'. You will note from the above chart that the market had begun to slip in the month before the crash and as such it was not an unforeseeable event to the perceptive. As the market began to slip, the level of discomfort amongst investors would have been building and professional investors would have been easing out of some positions. I say 'some' because all market participants were caught up in the euphoria of the uptrend and my experience was that prior to the crash the market was drifting back in a retracement, not an active profit-taking purge. I know of not one member of the overpaid funds management community that avoided the crash.

Trends are not infinite and they come to an end eventually. The market of October '87 was running out of buyers. To sustain itself a bull market needs a constant supply of new money, it needs individuals who had not previously been buyers to enter the market. New buyers were a diminishing resource which was eventually exhausted. Gradually sellers began to gain the ascendancy as they had done in late September and early October. As the selling accelerated the trend broke and the spiral of competition began. Any reasons for the crash and subsequent bear market are merely justifications for the overwhelming herd mentality that grips markets. Once the selling starts, panic spreads throughout the investing public with extraordinary speed. If you doubt the ability of crowds to respond like a shoal of fish, try a little experiment next time you are crossing the road. Instead of strolling across the road, jog—I can guarantee you half the crowd crossing the road will start to run for no other reason than the fact you are running.

A bear market, then, begins as the general investing public—who have the least tolerance for risk—scramble to get out of the market. The general public, aware of the damage they have been done by the market, shy away from it, until a new generation of investors emerges.

TRENDLINES

Trendlines are often an overlooked tool in a trader's arsenal. As traders search for ever-more-powerful tools they tend to ignore how much information can be gathered by a chart, a pencil and a ruler. A simple trendline on a chart will convey instantly most of the information about a given instrument that you will need to know. As you would expect a trendline is merely a line connecting several points on a chart.

In a rising market a line is drawn connecting the lows and in a falling market a line is drawn connecting the highs. The drawing of trendlines in its most simple form can be seen in the following chart of the Commonwealth Bank.

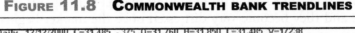

FIGURE 11.8 COMMONWEALTH BANK TRENDLINES

In drawing trendlines there is some debate among technical analysts as to the conventions to be used when deciding which points to include. Traditionalists insist that there should be a strict adherence to the convention of, for example, joining all the highs and lows, making certain to include the most extreme prices. This approach is rather like joining the dots. The second approach, which has been popularised by noted trader Victor Sperandeo, is to exclude the extreme values you may get at the end of a trend and connect the trendline to the lowest low of the move and to the highest minor low prior to the next high. Sperandeo insists that this approach will cut through the congestion at the end of trends and identify a change in trend.

As with most things in trading common sense is the only rule you should use. In drawing a trendline it is only necessary to get the major parts of a move in. Most frequently these major price swings will be set early in the life of the trend and all subsequent price action will be a reflection of these points. More often than not a trendline may only have two or three points of contact with the price. One of the problems with many purists is that they do not actually trade. What they do is spend an inordinate amount of time sitting in front of their screens playing with their computer packages. They often spend hours constructing beautifully organised charts that have the right mix of colours and indicators. Unfortunately the market does not often agree with the clinical beauty of such charts. Granted markets are beautiful and they can display a remarkable synchronicity but they are often a little dirty and a little untidy. Trends can be the same, so don't get terribly concerned about the drawing of trendlines.

Any approach needs to be objective. Too many traders try to draw their trendlines so they reflect their bias about the market; such an approach is self-defeating. If we suspect that our biases are creeping into our analysis, we should print the chart and then turn it upside-down and draw our trendlines. Inverting the chart throws off our perception and forces us to analyse what we see, not what we want to see.

Traders often cover their charts with so many lines that the resultant image starts to look like an aerial photograph of the Melbourne tram network. In drawing trendlines, simple is best. There is nothing wrong with gradually building up your analysis but you must get the underlying trend correct before you start to fine tune.

Do not be afraid to run your trends through zones of congestion. These areas are a very valuable signpost and a boldly drawn trendline will often make sense of very volatile price action.

It is very easy to draw trendlines on the left-hand side of a chart. Unfortunately we cannot trade the left-hand side of our chart, we have to trade against the right-hand margin. Drawing beautiful trendlines that highlight trends of six months ago often does not help us with today's trading decisions.

What is a Trendline Telling Us?

Trendlines don't just tell us of the direction of the market. They are not simply arrows saying follow me, this way up or down. Trendlines give us an insight into the emotional intensity of the market via their longevity. The longevity of a trend gives us an idea of the level of force behind a move. It displays the commitment of the dominant market group to the move.

Time is the key in determining the strength of a trend; the longer it has been in force the greater the influence on the possible future direction of price. An understanding of time also leads to a number of possible trading scenarios. Firstly if a trend has been in place for a relatively long period of time based upon the timeframe with which you view the market then any counter-trend reversal is simply a sign to enter the stock. If you are already in the position then these reversals offer an opportunity to pyramid into the position.

Secondly a trend that has enjoyed some degree of longevity will eventually end. When it does it will be a major reversal, thereby allowing you to trade the break of the trend aggressively. Such scenarios can be examined by viewing the following chart of AMP.

FIGURE 11.9 AMP TRENDS

124

During the period in question the predominant trend for AMP was down. If you were a portfolio trader and you were long the stock at any stage during this move you were wrong.

Such a scenario offered several trading opportunities:

1. Portfolio traders or those with a long-term point of view could have been out of the stock, thereby saving the trauma of watching it decay.

2. For those who had a more aggressive profile the small accelerations in downtrend that occurred in March and May offered an opportunity to either short sell the stock or engage in some form of derivatives trade.

3. The counter-trend reversal offered a small upside trade either through purchasing the stock or derivatives.

4. The reversal from this move up once again offered a chance to short the stock.

The downtrend in AMP did not end in a straight reversal, rather a period of congestion. When the stock did break this period of congestion it accelerated upwards in price (see below).

FIGURE 11.10   AMP UPTREND

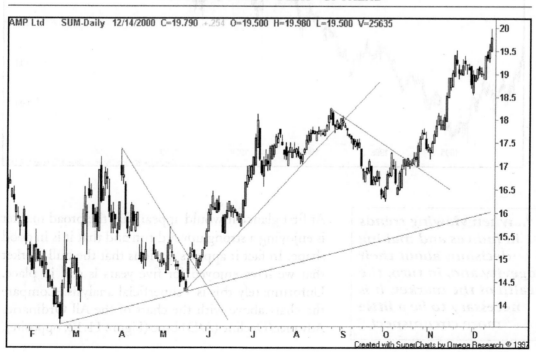

We have almost the mirror image of the breakdown that characterised AMP in Figure 11.9. As the stock lifted from congestion we had a predominant uptrend with a series of counter-trend reversals.

However when viewing trends in indices and making decisions about their longevity and, in turn, the health of the market, it is necessary to be a little more circumspect. For example, consider this chart of the All Ordinaries Index.

FIGURE 11.11   ALL ORDINARIES

At first glance it would appear that the broad market is enjoying a strong upward run and that it is in good shape. In fact it appears obvious that the bull market that we have enjoyed for five years is still in place. Unfortunately this is a superficial analysis. Compare the chart above with the chart of the All Ordinaries Advance/Decline (A/D) Line (Figure 11.12, opposite).

> *"...when viewing trends in indices and making decisions about their longevity and, in turn, the health of the market, it is necessary to be a little more circumspect."*

126

FIGURE 11.12 ALL ORDINARIES ADVANCE/DECLINE

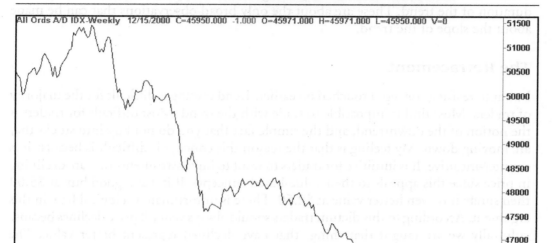

The A/D line gives traders an idea of the number of stocks going up versus the number going down. What can clearly be seen from this comparison is that the All Ordinaries Index peaked in 1997, almost two years before the collapse of the Nasdaq and the subsequent market turmoil. The reason the All Ordinaries Index continued to climb is that it is a weighted index; a small number of stocks exert a disproportionate influence on the direction of the index. This situation is heightened due to the impact of News Corp., which at its peak can comprise over 20% of the Australian market.

In trading it pays to look beyond the obvious.

Trend Slopes

Before I leave this part of the discussion I need to mention something about the slope of the trend. In many methodologies much is made about the number of degrees a trend is moving up by and the number of days it has been in force. Unfortunately such concepts are nonsense. You can only make some very superficial judgements about the slope of a trend because of the simple fact that the slope is scale-dependent. Change the scale and the slope changes dramatically, thereby invalidating any conclusions you have made.

The only way you can make any judgement regarding slope is to make a broad assessment based upon consistent observation, and even then you have to be careful. The broad observations are the more aggressive an upward or downward move the shorter the move will be. Conversely the gentler the apparent move the longer the duration of the trend. These are about the only broad observations that can be made about the slope of the trend.

The Retracement

I want to revisit a concept I touched on earlier. Trend trading is difficult for the majority of traders. Most find it impossible to trade with the trend. Most difficult for traders is the notion of the downtrend, and the simple fact that you do not buy into stocks that are moving down. My feeling is that the reason this concept is difficult is because it is counter-intuitive. It is intuitive for traders to want to buy instruments that are declining in price since this appeals to their value-based concepts. If it was a good buy at $5.00 then surely it is even better value at $2.50. There is unfortunately a logical flaw in this argument. According to this dictum traders should always wait till price declines because culturally we are taught that things that have declined represent better value. The more they decline the better value they are. The problem with this notion is that if we take it to a logical conclusion then we should always wait until price reaches zero before buying because at this point the stock has infinite value.

Likewise it is intuitive for traders not to want to buy instruments that are moving up in price, particularly if they have come from a low base. Surely you can't want to buy a stock that has gone from $2.50 to $5.00? That's a 100% increase, therefore the stock must be overvalued.

Price, however, is an irrelevant notion, as are concepts of value. To reinforce this consider the two charts opposite, which continue to defy the notion of relative value.

Whilst these two charts are extreme cases what they illustrate is the market's complete disregard for personal opinions. As I mentioned in the psychology section the market really doesn't care what you think. Markets are wonderfully non-discriminatory—they don't care what anyone thinks.

The question then arises of how to treat those times when the prevailing trend does falter, since this represents a time of both opportunity and danger. The danger is that traders will fall into the trap of wanting to trade markets in an intuitive manner, so they will see small reversals in a downtrend as proof of a buying opportunity and confirmation of their notions of value. As such they will be tempted to buy into a downtrend.

Conversely during an uptrend a trader who holds a stock may see a counter-trend reversal as confirmation of a belief in a stock being overvalued and therefore may sell the stock pre-emptively.

FIGURE 11.13 COCHLEAR

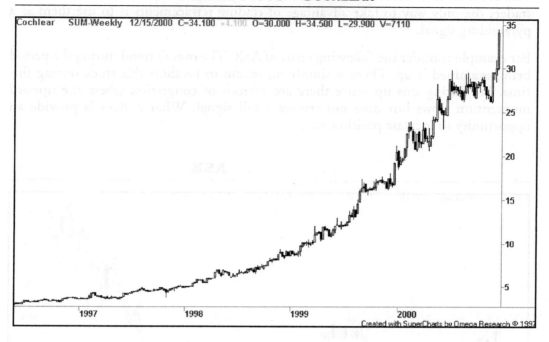

Cochlear SUM-Weekly 12/15/2000 C=34.100 +4.100 O=30.000 H=34.500 L=29.900 V=7110

Created with SuperCharts by Omega Research ® 1997

FIGURE 11.14 CSL

CSL Limited SUM-Weekly 12/15/2000 C=38.430 +1.530 O=36.900 H=38.750 L=36.650 V=10245

Created with SuperCharts by Omega Research ® 1997

The question then becomes: how can these retracements be profited from? For most traders the only way to take advantage of trading retracements is to use them as a pyramiding signal.

For example consider the following chart of ASX. The overall trend during the period being examined is up. There is simply no reason to be short this stock during this time. Yet during this up move there are periods of congestion where the upward momentum slows but does not trigger a sell signal. What it does is provide an opportunity to increase position size.

FIGURE 11.15 ASX

In trying to trade counter-trend reversals I want to make a fairly blunt point. Trying to trade against the major trend is a fool's game. As the above chart shows trading in the direction of the primary trend is the only avenue for success. Trying to trade against this is next to useless.

If you are a highly aggressive trader who trades narrow timeframes then you can trade small movements in the market. But given that you are used to trading small time periods and that this narrow focus is the style of market you operate in you are not really trading reversals, merely a shorter trend that is reflective of your style of trading.

Eventually however a counter-trend reversal becomes a full-blown reversal. The trick is in spotting the emergence of the new trend. This recognition can come in the following ways. Firstly, if you are, say, long a stock and your stop is triggered then it is fairly obvious that the probability of the trend ending is high. Secondly, with this a move through a major trendline or other trend-following instrument, such as a moving average, may occur. The move must be marked and significant; noise doesn't count as a reversal of trend.

Trend and Volume

Trend and volume are inseparable. Volume can confirm or deny the validity of a trend. It is a measure of the emotional commitment of the underlying herd to any given move. Confirmation is apparent when volume increases as prices move in the direction of a trend and decreases when prices drift back towards the trendline.

If we return to the example of ASX and this time include volume (see Figure 11.16, below), we can see the confirming nature of volume in breakouts. Volume decreases as price moves back to the underlying trend and then lifts as new participants move into the market.

FIGURE 11.16 ASX WITH VOLUME

The reasoning for this renewal is quite simple; as prices move in tandem with the trend market participants feel that their decisions to trade in a particular direction are justified and are therefore willing to participate in any movement that appears to confirm their view. As prices drift away from the trend the level of anxiety felt by traders who are already committed to the trend rises and they are unwilling to participate in the decline. Traders have a tendency to ignore any information that does not confirm their underlying bias. If they are long the market they will ignore any drift back. If they are short the market they ignore any price rises. In this respect traders have a lot in common with ostriches. This situation will persist until the underlying psychology of the market changes and the prevailing group faces exhaustion, leaving the way clear for a change in emotional momentum.

Put simply a trend will persist until everyone who wishes, for example, to be long the underlying instrument is committed to their position. This is reflected in the explosion of volume in the early stages of a move. This lift in volume confirms the move. Volume then settles down to what could loosely be termed normal activity. At the top of the move there is a lift in volume as the last of the bulls commit themselves. This is generally the phase at which amateurs pour into the market and take on enormous risk. All of the buyers are now fully committed to the move—there is simply no one to keep the momentum going. Sellers then creep into the market. At first this selling is merely a reflection of normal market activity—it is by no means forced selling. However all the bulls are committed to the move so there is no one to absorb the selling, and prices slip. As they slip many of the amateurs who got in at the top of the move begin to panic and compete with one another for the few available buyers. Since the only mechanism of competition in the market is price sellers continually lower their asking price in order to exit their positions. As a result a top forms and the trend reverses.

> *"...as prices move in tandem with the trend market participants feel that their decisions to trade in a particular direction are justified..."*

Part IV

INDICATORS

"The victorious army wins first and then seeks battle."

Sun Tzu, The Art of War, *6th Century BC*

12

MOVING AVERAGES

WHEN EXAMINING TRENDLINES we simply plotted a series of straight lines against the price action of a given instrument. The aim was to use the raw price action to identify any swings in sentiment. In looking at moving averages we are moving away from raw price as a means of making trading decisions. Up until this point our charts were unencumbered by analytical techniques. In using an indicator it is important to realise that some of the purity of price is being sacrificed for comfort. Indicators simply provide comfort to the trader. They are merely triggers to do something. They are not magic and you must not fall into the trap of believing that just because you are massaging the data you are increasing your chances of success. This is known as the lotto bias. To gain an insight into this form of bias, the next time you are in a newsagent watch people as they fill in lottery coupons. By and large they do this by hand. They do this because of a belief that they are exerting some control over a random event. Humans always seek constancy in uncertain times. Anything that can be done to provide a balm against uncertainty will be done.

Remember that indicators, their construction and interpretation make up probably less than 10% of a trader's life. This is a theme I will return to several times during this section. Indicators will not provide certainty. They will not insulate you against your own stupidity or laziness, but they may give you just enough confidence in yourself to act.

In using moving averages we employ a similar technique to trendlines except that we apply a smoothing technique to the actual price data and plot that against the price action of whatever we are trading. In essence, we are trying to filter out some of the noise that surrounds the movements in price that all instruments display. This filtering gives a smooth line that is merely, as you would expect from the name, an average of the accumulated price data for the underlying commodity.

The construction of moving averages does require some computation. Those of you who are not mathematically inclined have no need to panic, computers do all the number-crunching these days. The only calculations you will be exposed to here are by way of example. For those of you who are keen to calculate your own moving averages—*don't*. It is a complete waste of time and effort.

Types of Moving Averages

Moving averages can be divided into three broad categories:

- Simple moving average (SMA)
- Exponential moving average (EMA)
- Weighted moving average (WMA).

The differences arise due to the method of calculation employed. Simple moving averages are, as their name implies, merely an average of a given number of days' trading. As such they give equal weight to all data. This poses a problem for traders since the moving average changes when new data is added and when an old price is dropped off. These changes in the moving average have nothing to do with the price change in the underlying commodity but are rather a response to the method of calculation. As such the trader is getting a false image. What you see is not quite a true reflection of reality. Although this does present some problems its importance is generally overstated by technical analysts. There are instances where a simple moving average may be more effective than either of the more complex alternatives.

The formula for calculating simple moving averages is as follows:

$$\text{Simple Moving Average} = \frac{P_1 + P_2 + P_3 + P_4 \dots P_n}{N}$$

where: P = price that is being averaged

N = number of days in the moving average

A simple moving average is shown in Figure 12.1 (opposite).

FIGURE 12.1 18-DAY SIMPLE MOVING AVERAGE

Australia DolSFE-Daily 12/12/2000 C=54.070 -.560 O=54.200 H=54.200 L=53.970 V=0 Mov Avg 1 line

Created with SuperCharts by Omega Research ® 1997

Exponential moving averages employ a different method of calculation. This calculation gives greater weight to the current data being input and therefore responds faster to changes in trend than a simple moving average, although it should be noted that the effect of the first piece of data in the data stream can never be eliminated fully. An exponential moving average is shown in Figure 12.2 (overleaf). For those who are interested, the exponential moving average is calculated as follows:

$$\text{Exponential Moving Average} = (P_t \times K) + EMA_y \times (1 - K)$$

$$\text{where: } K = \frac{2}{N + 1}$$

N = number of days in the moving average

P_t = today's price

EMA_y = yesterday's EMA

Weighted moving averages are similar to exponential moving averages in that they attempt to eliminate the influence of old data and heighten the effect of recent price fluctuations in order to get a more rapid response to changes in trend. This is achieved by assigning an arbitrary weighting factor to new data since it is assumed that what happened five days ago is of less importance than what happened yesterday. A weighted moving average is shown in 12.3 (overleaf).

FIGURE 12.2   18-DAY EXPONENTIAL MOVING AVERAGE

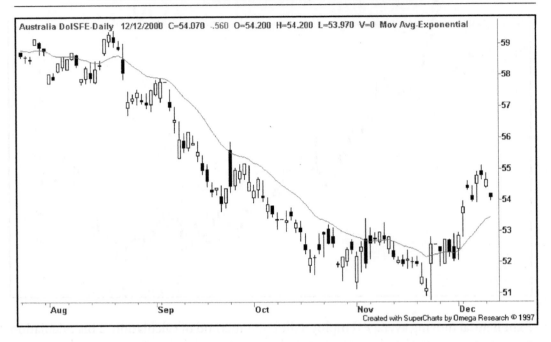

FIGURE 12.3   18-DAY WEIGHTED MOVING AVERAGE

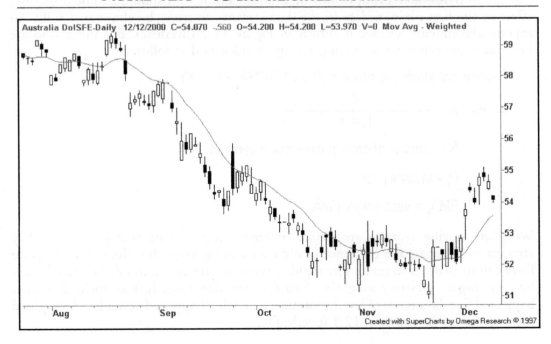

A quick glance at these charts shows something remarkable—all three moving averages head down when price is heading down and all three head up when price is heading up. This is somewhat of a revelation to traders who continually play with various moving average types. Moving averages are a trend-following tool. Their construction is irrelevant—they will always be trend-following.

The simple moving average, exponential moving average and weighted moving average have similar tracks through the price action. The major difference arises during periods of sideways trading. The exponential and weighted moving averages flatten out more quickly, thereby perhaps alerting the trader to slack periods, although this point is debatable.

This brings me to a drawback in the use of moving averages. They are not an end in themselves but are part of the trader's arsenal. Many traders are seduced by the effectiveness of moving averages and there is no doubting their usefulness. In trendless markets, however, they are next to useless; during these periods traders need to rely on other tools.

Selecting Moving Average Timeframes

Moving averages, like all trend-following tools, require traders to specify what time period they are interested in since they are time-specific. There is no point trying to trade exchange traded options or futures whilst using a 200-day moving average. Conversely, there is no rationale behind the decision to make long-term portfolio trades using an 8-day moving average.

Traders go through all sorts of mental gyrations looking for the right combination of moving averages. Most software programs come with what are called 'optimisation' programs that allow the back-testing of moving averages, either singly or in combination. I am a fan of testing trading methods as you will see later in the book, however optimisation is based on the assumption that what worked yesterday will work today and perhaps more importantly tomorrow. Logically, this would seem so, but unfortunately this is not the entire story. The market changes over time and the tools required to trade it must also evolve. You will not find a magic combination of moving averages that will guarantee you fame and fortune, but this does not diminish their effectiveness in providing a mental crutch for the trader to lean on.

The choice of moving average term is a reflection of the timeframe that you want to trade. You should be clear in your own mind as to the reasons why you want to trade, and what timeframe you are interested in trading. This will provide the foundation for your trader's business plan. It is also the key that unlocks the timeframe for which moving averages you use. If you wish to be an aggressive intraday trader then you will most likely look at tick data and use moving averages that are measured in minutes. The chart on the following page is a chart of the SPI with a 15-minute weighted moving average drawn through it.

FIGURE 12.4 SPI WITH MOVING AVERAGE

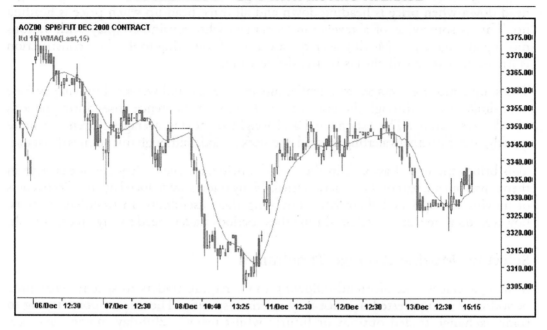

As you would expect its shape and tone are no different to moving averages that are placed over longer time periods. It should be obvious that if you are going to trade an instrument such as the SPI intraday then any trigger you use should reflect this. It would be foolish trying to trade the SPI intraday using very long periods over your intraday data.

Conversely consider portfolio traders who may only make a few adjustments to their superannuation fund each year. Such traders would look at weekly data since they would not be interested in the day-to-day noise that accompanies markets. Such an approach may require a mid-term moving average, such as between 15 and 20 weeks (see Figure 12.5, opposite). Figure 12.5 has an 18-week moving average.

> *"In choosing which moving averages to use the only prerequisite is that desperately rare commodity, common sense."*

In choosing which moving averages to use the only prerequisite is that desperately rare commodity, common sense. There is no such thing as a magic moving average. There is no magical type of moving average nor is there a magical moving average number. There are simply moving average types and timeframes that reflect your approach to markets. They are tools that merely reflect how you want to trade—nothing more, nothing less.

140

FIGURE 12.5   NAB WITH MOVING AVERAGE

Nat. Bank   SUM-Weekly   12/15/2000 C=29.200 -.383 O=29.600 H=29.600 L=29.020 V=57459

Created with SuperCharts by Omega Research © 1997

Moving Averages as a Trading Tool

After discussing the nitty gritty of the assembling of moving averages, what values to use and their advantages and disadvantages, it's time to focus on how they can be employed to generate some trading rules.

Traditionally moving averages have been used in one of two ways as a trading tool; they have been be used singly or in a variety of combinations. However, lately a disturbing trend has gathered force, and that is the plastering of what are known as 'multiple moving averages' all over the underlying price chart. The philosophy seems to be that if one moving average is a good thing then 32 must be a really good thing. I have great difficulties with this approach for two reasons. It suspiciously resembles a desperate attempt to find a Holy Grail, and is a terrible over-manipulation of the data. Again the quest for certainty has tainted the analysis with complexity. Trading is a simple endeavour and it needs to be treated as such.

I am an advocate of the use of single moving averages. These averages must be reflective of the timeframe you trade and the data you use to trade. Used singly moving averages spot major breaks in trend; combinations simply give us a confirmation of a break in trend. The deadliest system I have ever come across is a weighted moving average overlaid onto closing prices. As an example consider the following chart (Figure 12.6, overleaf).

FIGURE **12.6** **NAB 18-**DAY WEIGHTED MOVING AVERAGE

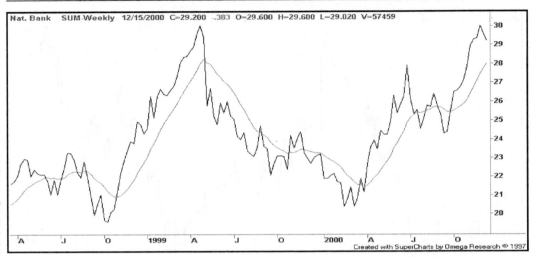

This is simply a weekly chart of NAB with closing prices plotted and an 18-week weighted moving average applied. Such a system would have caught every major swing in NAB in the past two years. Granted there are whipsaws or times when prices congested, but this is largely irrelevant since moving averages serve only as a trigger. They get you into the trade.

As we have discussed the hard part is done before the trade begins (deciding your position sizing) and whilst the trade is being managed, so that you exit on reversal signals when they come (see Figure 12.7, opposite). Using a simple system you would have caught the dead cat bounce in Sausage (SAS) in mid-1999 and been short the stock for most of the remainder of the year. You would not have been swept up like the rest of the wood ducks in the belief that the tech market had bottomed.

Entering a Trade

If you have decided on your system the major question is: when do you enter? Many traders set penetration limits to try and avoid whipsaws. Traders decide that they will enter a trade if the moving average is penetrated by 2%, 3%, 5% or whatever figure they choose. Such decisions are purely arbitrary. Setting a time-based trigger may also be effective; for example, if a stock or commodity closes either side of the moving average for two days in succession then a new position can be opened.

There are a few subtleties that need to be understood with moving averages. The first revolves around using them as pyramiding signals. Often during the life of a stock or commodity, price will move back towards the underlying moving average and then accelerate again. Such a situation can be seen in the Figure 12.8 (opposite).

FIGURE 12.7   SAS WITH MOVING AVERAGE

FIGURE 12.8   ASX WITH MOVING AVERAGE

As can be seen the price makes a number of counter-trend reversals, moving back to the moving average and then bouncing off it. These are signals to pyramid into a trade. They are not signals to exit a position.

Exiting a Trade

The second subtlety concerns the limited utility of moving averages as an exit strategy. Moving averages can be thought of as a consensus of value as determined by the underlying herd. Occasionally price will move away from this consensus value in a rapid explosion. Such explosions are unsustainable but they do offer the chance to profit. For an example consider the following chart.

FIGURE 12.9   METALSTORM MOVEMENT

Metalstorm exploded out of a long period of consolidation, as can be seen. Price rapidly moved away from the moving average only to retrace quite sharply. If you had been relying on the moving average to provide both an entry and an exit signal you would have been disappointed by the results that were achieved during this trade.

Price will always regress to the mean. In practical terms the feelings of the crowd dominate so when prices move explosively away from the moving average they then will always move back to this mean consensus of value. As a consequence of this, explosive moves will catch traders who use moving averages for exits unawares. Such moves are better exited using a volatility measure such as ATR, or a percentage drawdown from a peak or a move below a significant previous bar.

A Wider Perspective

At any given time the market can be a mixture of trends, all co-existing. In reality trends are like wheels within wheels. Traders often adopt a narrow focus when they are involved in trading the market on a fairly regular basis. To myopic traders all that exists is today and what trade they may or may not undertake. Such an approach cuts traders off from valuable sources of information.

Moving averages can be plotted on weekly and monthly charts. By doing this traders are placing their trading activity in the context of the overall movements in the market. This is necessary because a trader who watches the market on a

> *"At any given time the market can be a mixture of trends, all co-existing."*

daily basis may not be aware of the full significance of a given move if that move changes a trend that has existed for months or even years. To overcome this traders should view the market through a variety of timeframes.

When *Not* to Use Moving Averages

By definition, moving averages are a trend-following tool. They are at their most effective when the market is trending either up or down. In a drifting market they are largely useless. As a general rule, traders should look to other indicators during flat markets. If your moving average has flattened out and is effectively linear discount the breakouts it gives you and rely during this period on other indicators.

MOVING AVERAGE CONVERGENCE DIVERGENCE (MACD)

13

AS ITS NAME SUGGESTS, the MACD is merely a mechanism for plotting the difference between a series of moving averages. Whilst the construction of the MACD requires three moving averages to be calculated only two appear on the screen. These are known as the fast MACD line, and the slower line as the signal line. In addition, a third unit is plotted, the MACD histogram, which is the result of subtracting the MACD line from the signal line.

To manually create a MACD you would undertake the following steps:

1. Calculate a 13-day exponential moving average.

2. Calculate a 21-day exponential moving average.

3. Subtract the 21-day exponential moving average from the 13-day exponential moving average. This difference is then plotted.

4. Calculate an 8-day exponential moving average of the fast line.

An example of the MACD can be seen in Figure 13.1 (overleaf).

FIGURE 13.1   **NAB** MACD

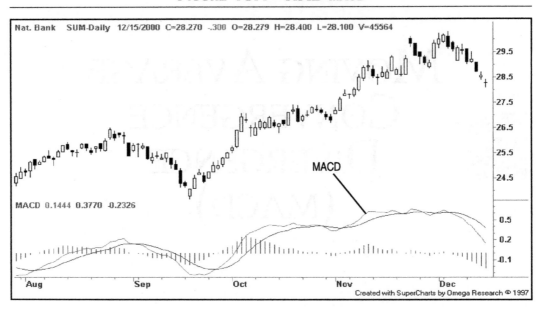

Nat. Bank   SUM-Daily 12/15/2000 C=28.270 -.300 O=28.279 H=28.400 L=28.100 V=45564

This is simply a variation on the moving average crossover theme that most traders should be familiar with. When the signal line drops below the MACD line a buy signal is generated. When the reverse occurs and the signal line moves above the MACD line a sell signal is generated.

There is also a third signal that can be given by the MACD. We have touched on it briefly before and it is one of the most powerful signals in the market. If the two moving averages in a MACD touch but do not cross then traders have been given a signal to lift their level of involvement in a given position.

The designer of the MACD, Gerald Appel, has stated that it is his belief that the MACD works better in bull markets than bear markets. My own experience is that this is true only to a point. The MACD is extremely sensitive to the underlying trend, hence it responds well to any oscillation in sentiment. However, traders should be aware that the MACD often picks up signals that offer no trading opportunity since they may be very small windows of opportunity.

Before acting on MACD signals, traders should be aware of the prevailing major trend in the market. If the market is moving very strongly in a given direction then any contrary signal from the MACD should be viewed carefully. It should not be discarded out of hand, since it is obviously highlighting the ebbs and flows in sentiment, but you should be aware that it may only be a transient sign of a very small shift in sentiment.

148

It would be wiser to wait for further confirmation before committing to a trade that ran against the prevailing trend.

A falling MACD may actually indicate a possible slowing or breakdown in the market. Likewise a rising MACD in a bear market may signal a slowing of the slippage or a complete reversal. We need to be aware of what the broader trend is before taking any action otherwise we will get caught by a series of false breaks which will chew up our equity and our patience. Remember, no indicator works in isolation of common sense.

MACD Timeframes

The MACD requires that traders select which timeframes they wish to input. This is only logical since the MACD is a tool that is dependent upon moving averages for its construction.

In constructing a MACD the same rules that applied to moving averages hold true. Short-term traders will want to use a series of moving averages that reflect their interest in daily trading, whereas longer-term averages are useful in spotting more significant changes in trend. There is no magic combination that unlocks the secrets of the market. The selection of appropriate timeframes is largely a matter of compromise. You want to be able to trade relatively small swings in the markets without being whipped in and out or missing the significant changes in trend.

"There is no magic combination that unlocks the secrets of the market."

The fact that the MACD can be used on a weekly or even monthly scale to reinforce in the trader's mind the significance of trend changes is often ignored. A MACD signal on a weekly basis is a significant event that a trader needs to be aware of. It is pointless trying to trade swings in the trend if the market is changing tack on a timeframe that you do not even consider. It pays to watch the longer-term trends in the market simply to be aware of in which overall direction the market is headed.

Histogram

The MACD histogram is a refinement on the simple viewing of a pair of moving averages. The histogram portion of the chart (which is shown in Figure 13.1) through which the two moving averages move conveys an enormous amount of information about the strength of the underlying trend and it warns traders of any possible shift in sentiment.

It is impossible to predict the future. The aim of analysing the MACD histogram is not to attempt such a foolish stunt but rather to aid us in gathering intelligence about the state of the trading universe. Consider what I am about to talk about next as the trading equivalent of sticking your head out the window to see what the weather might be. You may see clouds on the horizon and assume it is going to rain. The clouds, though, may not co-operate with you. They may pass you by. They may disperse before they get to you. Examining the MACD histogram is the same—just because you think it will happen does not mean it has to happen.

Remember you have absolutely no control over the market. If you happen to go in the same direction as the market this is a good thing but it is merely coincidence. The market was going to go in the direction it chose to go with or without you.

In the chart below I have deleted the signal lines and shown only the histogram. What can be seen is that NAB is making a series of higher highs and higher lows. This is the primary trend and this is of enormous importance to us in our decision-making. Nothing else matters. Personal feelings are irrelevant. Opinions are irrelevant. What your broker thinks is irrelevant. The trend is all that matters.

FIGURE 13.2 **NAB** HISTOGRAM

However there is a subtlety to this picture that needs to be examined. As NAB is tracking up, the MACD histogram is trending down. This gives us a clue that whilst the trend may be moving up perhaps the underlying herd is not as committed to the move as it may initially seem. This is known as a Type 1 bearish divergence. I will examine divergences in greater detail in the next chapter. What these apparent dislocations between price and sentiment tell us is that the trend is weakening. It lacks support as each move to a new high is met with less enthusiasm. This is only logical since as stock prices move higher cultural notions of value take over and traders feel they are getting less and less of a bargain, and that if a stock has moved up by any significant amount then it surely cannot be as good value as it once was. As such their commitment to the trend wanes.

Do not under any circumstances ignore the primary trend. If the trend is up go long. If the trend is down go short. Remember using the MACD is the equivalent of sticking your head out the window, nothing more. You are not developing some great sage-like ability to predict the future.

As divergences unfold you may wish to develop some stop loss modifications to deal with them. For example, as a long-term trend-follower you may have an ATR-based stop that is 2.5ATR from the recent highest high. At the sign of the first divergence you may move this to 2.0ATR. As the second divergence unfolds this stop may be moved to 1.5ATR.

You may wish to develop some form of position-sizing model to deal with the emergence of a divergence. For example, you may have a 2% initial risk premium and a loose stop that allows for a 5% risk. As the divergence unfolds you may choose to lighten the position so that you are carrying no more than 2% risk. This is simply a variation of the theme I mentioned in the money management section.

There is no magic to the unfolding of divergences and the MACD histogram. It is merely the market showing you a potential signpost—nothing more, nothing less. The successful trading of them once again revolves around risk and its management.

14 LINEAR REGRESSION AND THE ADVANCE/DECLINE LINE

LINEAR REGRESSION IS simply a method whereby a line is plotted through the price of a security in an attempt to minimise the distance between the line and each individual point. The method used to achieve this is known as the 'least squares method'; in lay terms this is simply the line of best fit. In generating a linear regression line we are drawing a line through the price data so that the line passes through as many of the prices as possible. Linear regression is based upon the theory that there is an underlying force that will drag prices back to the regression line when they stray too far above or below the line.

Notice how in the chart of the 50 Leaders Index (see Figure 14.1, overleaf) the 21-day linear regression line hugs the share price data. Linear regression can be used on its own to enhance our perception of a trend and any deviation from it. However, it is most useful when combined with an additional trend-following tool such as a weighted moving average (see Figure 14.2, overleaf).

This method is interpreted in exactly the same manner as our standard moving averages.

FIGURE 14.1   FIFTY LEADERS WITH LINEAR REGRESSION

FIGURE 14.2   FIFTY LEADERS WITH LINEAR REGRESSION AND WMA

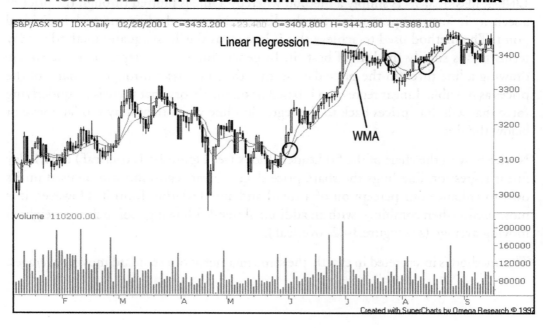

A cross in the upward direction is a bullish signal whereas a cross in the downward direction is bearish. It should be noted that because linear regression produces a trend that mimics very closely the underlying trend, timeframes of less than 13 days are practically useless as an analytical technique. Short timeframes produce a trend that is identical to the underlying trend with very little smoothing effect. The end result is a trend that reflects all the noise inherent in price movement. As such the trendline responds to every small jump in price thereby whipping the trader in and out of trades.

It is worth noting that many software packages are advertised on the basis of containing a special moving average that is more responsive to market moves than any of the forms of moving average that have been examined. Such a special or 'proprietary' moving average, as it is often referred to, is more than likely a form of linear regression.

The Advance/Decline Line

The advance/decline line is without doubt one of the most powerful tools available to traders. A trader needs to be able to spot changes in the underlying emotion of the market; simply knowing that some prices are going up and some are coming down tells a trader very little. Such information is a natural feature of markets.

The advance/decline line is, in effect, a measure of the confidence of the underlying market participants. It shows whether more stocks are advancing than declining. If this is the situation then the advance/decline line is positive. If more stocks are declining than advancing then the advance/decline line is negative.

The All Ordinaries advance/decline line is shown in Figure 14.3 (overleaf). It is quite meaningless to the trader on its own. To be relevant it needs to be compared to the All Ordinaries Index to gain an idea of the correlation between the two and to define whether the advance/decline line is a leading or lagging indicator.

The advance/decline line can be subjected to exactly the same form of analysis as any other collection of price data. In this instance I have compared a MACD histogram on the All Ordinaries advance/decline line with the All Ordinaries.

"The advance/decline line is without doubt one of the most powerful tools available to traders. A trader needs to be able to spot changes in the underlying emotion of the market..."

FIGURE 14.3 ALL ORDS ADVANCE/DECLINE

FIGURE 14.4 ALL ORDS ADVANCE/DECLINE

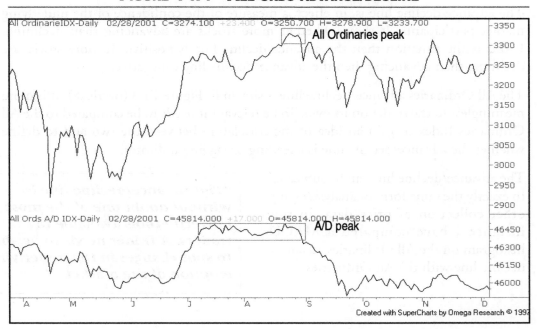

From the chart shown in Figure 14.4 (previous page) there are a number of observations which can be made:

⮑ The shape of these two lines is not analogous. The peaks and troughs of the advance/decline line do not correspond with those of the line chart of the All Ordinaries.

⮑ The advance/decline line peaks sooner than the All Ordinaries. Price rises in the All Ordinaries continue for slightly longer than in the advance/decline line.

⮑ The advance/decline line, when subjected to analysis, provides trading signals earlier than the All Ordinaries.

The fact that the advance/decline line is a leading indicator can be used to advantage by traders since they are given early warning of a change in trend. The mechanism of this early warning is obvious since as a move deteriorates fewer and fewer stocks are participating in the trend. The logic is that as an uptrend comes to an end, fewer and fewer larger stocks are advancing relative to the number declining. The number of advances is still sufficient to carry the All Ordinaries higher on simple inertia. This problem does not apply to the advance/decline line since its construction highlights the relative number of advances and declines.

As traders we would take note of the signal given by the advance/decline analysis and wind back any long positions that were in place. However, it must be noted that the time interval between a signal being generated and a response in the All Ordinaries is inconsistent, so traders will have to use an element of judgment in its interpretation. Despite this it is a powerful pre-emptive tool.

Divergence

There is a second method of generating signals from an advance/decline line and that is by observing the phenomenon known as 'divergence'. Divergence occurs when indicators that normally have a degree of correlation fail to follow one another. An example of divergence would be the All Ordinaries Index hitting a new high whilst the advance/decline line failed to hit a new high. The astute reader will have noticed that the advance/decline line can be subjected to all forms of analysis, including pattern recognition, trendlines, moving averages, etc., etc.

15   VOLUME

MANY TRADERS IGNORE volume on the rather erroneous assumption that it has no relevance to them so long as the price of their trade is heading in the right direction. The problem with this attitude is that it ignores the fact that volume is the driving force behind any market. Volume is literally a measure of the interaction between market participants; no volume means no traders, no traders means that any price action you see is largely irrelevant. It is the stock market equivalent of a mirage.

Volume determines how long a move in any direction will be sustained. It demonstrates the commitment of traders to the underlying move and it determines whether there is sufficient volume to exit a trade at a given price. It is completely irrelevant that a price may be heading in the direction of your trade if you cannot get out of your position. If you doubt me, ask someone who has been caught with what appears to be a winning options trade but is unable to liquidate the position because of a lack of volume.

When traders do look at volume as an indicator they often see only half the story. Volume is a positive indicator in that any market move accompanied by acceleration in volume is likely to be sustained. Most traders are familiar with this old axiom.

However, a move on a lack of volume is also an indicator. It is this facet of volume that traders often ignore. The presence of volume tells us something, but the lack of volume also tells us something. There is an old Japanese saying that to take no action is an action.

The chart of the Nasdaq in Figure 15.1 gives us some basic information on volume.

FIGURE 15.1 NASDAQ WITH VOLUME

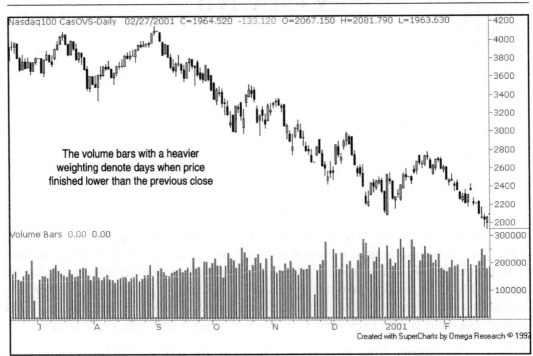

The volume bars with a heavier weighting denote days when price finished lower than the previous close

As you can see from the chart, volume on down days was higher than on the up days.

> *"It is not sufficient to merely look at a chart and try and divine some fact from a graphical representation of a particular stock or market."*

It is not sufficient to merely look at a chart and try and divine some fact from a graphical representation of a particular stock or market. Almost every time you look at the market you will have to perform some form of analysis, such as considering the ebbs and flows in the market's volume. Laziness will kill you as a trader.

Volume Declines

When volume declines during price falls it is a bullish signal. Such a situation may arise during retracements against the underlying trend. If these retracements occur on relatively low volume then this is a signal that the underlying trend is strong and that the bulls are still in control of the market. Traders would use the relatively lower prices that accompany these retracements to add to their long positions. As I have mentioned elsewhere, retracements are a normal part of market activity. Do not panic. Take advantage of the opportunities that such phenomena bring.

If volume declines during price rallies it is bearish. Such a development is typical of markets in the final phase of their uptrend. A change in trend is inevitable and traders should look to the short side of the market for profit opportunities.

Volume Rises

If volume rises during a period of price decline then this is a bearish signal. It indicates a substantial shift in the underlying sentiment in the market. It shows that the bears have sufficient energy not only to stop the momentum of the bulls but to actively turn the market around. Traders should roll up any long positions and go short.

When volume accelerates during price rises, it is a bullish signal. It shows that the bulls are firmly committed to the underlying trend and that buyers are plentiful. Traders would take long positions and definitely not try to short the market. In such a situation it is imperative that all short positions be closed.

Blowoffs and Climaxes

These are two of the more intriguingly-named volume-based phenomena that traders should be aware of. Blowoffs occur after a period of sharp price rises. Without warning the underlying trend will accelerate sharply. This acceleration is accompanied by a sharp rise in volume. This sudden lift is often accompanied by gaps in the price action.

The best way to describe blowoffs is by way of an analogy. They are the last sprint towards the line of a runner who is almost spent. We have all at some stage seen the situation of an athlete who makes a dash for the finish line throwing everything into one Herculean effort. A blowoff is no different. It is the last gasp of the bulls and a sign of an imminent reversal. This is shown in the chart overleaf.

At the apex of moves a massive form of risk transference takes place. As I mentioned before the top of a move can be characterised by a last-ditch panic assault by the bulls. The prevailing belief is that one of these may be the last up-move in a stock ever and if we don't buy this stock right now at this price then we will miss out forever. Clearly this is not true but no one ever said traders were rational.

FIGURE 15.2   SOLUTION 6 BLOWOFF

A curious thing happens at the top of the move. The last of the bulls are primarily amateurs or novice traders and they are entering at the time of greatest relative risk, yet they have the least understanding of risk and the damage it can do to them. It is commonplace for novices to buy into shares just as they reach their apogee. Professional traders have a quaint expression for this transference of risk. It is called feeding the chickens.

As the previous chart of Solution 6 (SOH) shows the largest volume day for the run in early July also coincided with the highest price for the remainder of the year. Novices and semi-professionals such as stockbrokers have flooded into the stock largely based upon a dead cat bounce and perceptions of relative value. It was once $18.00, it is now $4.00 so it must be better value now. The common question that is asked at these times is how much lower can it go? Well it can go all the way down to 84¢.

Large volume spikes at the relative tops of moves are something to be suspicious of simply because it means all the bulls are already committed to the move, therefore there is no one left to drive prices any higher and any selling is enough to swamp the remaining bulls and initiate a cascade of selling.

Climaxes

The opposite to a blowoff is a selling climax. Sellers begin what could only be described as panic-selling. They are willing to dump their positions at any price. In this situation the old homily of it being darkest before the dawn is correct. Selling climaxes shake the last of the stale bears out of the market. These traders have hung on and hung on and finally the pain of the market is too great and they dump their positions. Such a climax can be seen in Powertel (see Figure 15.3, overleaf).

Price had moved lower under the pressure of the bears as the technology shake-out of 1999 was in full swing. Volume accelerated in tandem with the falling price. This selling culminated in an enormous spike as the last of the bears were driven out of the market. The aggressiveness of the bulls was then sufficient to swamp the available selling and prices moved higher.

However as can be seen from this example it is impossible to gauge the longevity of a move simply by looking at the volume behind the move, as the bears soon moved back into ascendancy and prices moved substantially lower.

It is important to note that not every climax will cause a reversal of the prevailing trend. It is quite possible for buying or selling to climax and the trend to merely abate not reverse. This can be seen in Figure 15.4 (overleaf).

At the time of writing it appears as if the downtrend in SOH has ended. However, it did not end with a sudden reversal but rather a move into consolidation, as price is now congesting in a fairly narrow zone. This is not a bad thing in terms of future moves. Price can make very rapid advances from such zones. In effect they act as springboards for future upswings and it is very important that you develop a mental catalogue of stocks that are holding in such zones after prolonged moves down, since as time passes the balance of power will shift. In a zone of congestion the tone of the price is neutral—neither bulls nor bears are in charge—but this will change as one group, generally the bulls, gradually gains ascendancy. To illustrate the power of moves from congestion do a little homework on the moves technology stocks made when they ran towards their highs. What you will see is long periods of congestion followed by explosive moves.

On Balance Volume (OBV)

On Balance Volume (OBV) is a very neglected part of volume analysis. It represents a running tally of volume, hence it rises and falls each day depending on whether prices closed higher or lower than the day before. On balance volume attempts to determine the buying or selling pressure that is present in the market. If, as I said before, volume represents the emotional intensity of the dominant market group then OBV follows the involvement of traders in the market.

FIGURE 15.3 POWERTEL CLIMAX

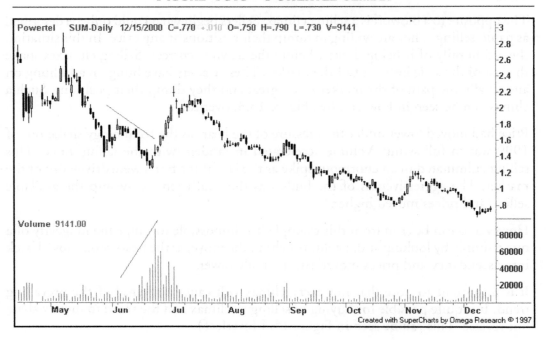

FIGURE 15.4 SOLUTION 6 CLIMAX

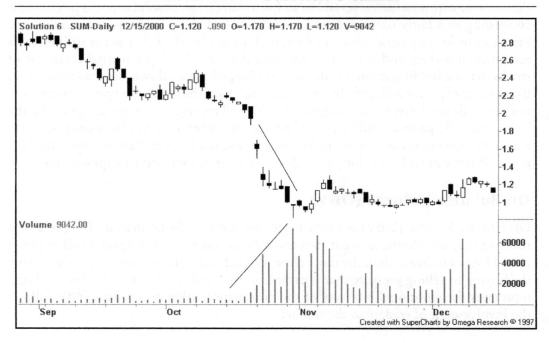

If OBV is rising then it shows that the bulls are in charge; if OBV is falling then the bears are in charge. This can be seen below.

FIGURE 15.5   NASDAQ WITH ON BALANCE VOLUME

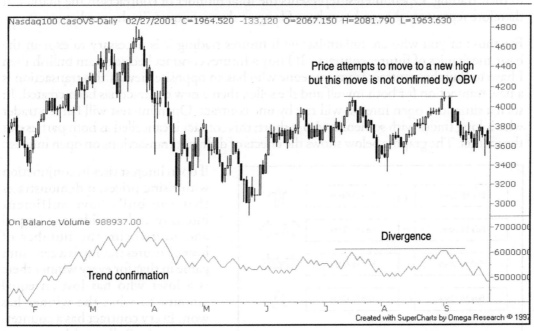

Taking Figure 15.5 as an example, we can see how trading signals are generated by the OBV in the following manner:

> *"If OBV is rising then it shows that the bulls are in charge; if OBV is falling then the bears are in charge."*

↪ When the trend of OBV and price are in harmony it confirms the strength of the trend. Whenever OBV and price have moved together, the underlying trend has persisted.

↪ When the OBV diverges from price it gives a signal to either buy or sell. Notice how in March 2000 prices attempted to pierce the most recent high whilst OBV was retreating, indicating a weakening in the power of the bulls.

↪ In April a bullish divergence was generated when OBV hit its low and then began to track up whereas prices went on to make another low before reversing.

Open Interest

If you trade any form of derivative you will be familiar with the term 'open interest'. Open interest figures are quoted beside the bid and offer spreads in the daily papers. Unfortunately most traders are startlingly unfamiliar with the concept of open interest and its relevance to their trading. Open interest represents the total number of contracts in the market. It therefore represents the total number of long or short contracts in the market.

For those of you who are unfamiliar with futures trading it is necessary to explain the basic mechanics of futures contracts. If I buy a futures contract because I am bullish then I have to buy this contract from someone who has an opposite view. If this transaction is a new transaction for both myself and the seller, then a new contract has been created. In such a situation, open interest will rise by one contract. Open interest will fall if a trader who is long trades with someone who is short; this contact is cancelled as both parties exit the market. The graphic below shows the effects of different transactions on open interest.

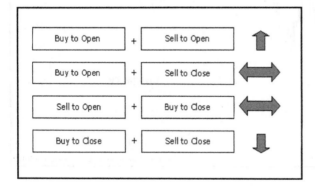

If open interest rises in conjunction with rising prices, it demonstrates that the bulls have sufficient intensity and confidence to equal and overwhelm the number of bears. Futures trading is a zero-sum game in that for every winner there is a loser who has lost an equal amount to what the winner has won. Every contract has a counter-party to it. Bulls and bears must match up for open interest to rise.

A rising trend in futures prices is assured as long as bears continue to flood the market in an attempt to pick the top and catch a reversal. The logic for an assumption of continually rising prices is that trends need new participants. As bears enter the market they are matched against the bulls. The bears perpetuate the uptrend by having to buy back their positions to cover them. As a result they push prices higher and higher.

Conversely, if open interest rises during a downtrend then it demonstrates that the bears are firmly in charge and are busy shorting the market whilst the bulls are attempting to pick the bottom. As prices decay the bulls exacerbate the trend by having to sell their positions to cover. So long as there is a new supply of bulls the trend is likely to continue.

Rising open interest during a trend is confirmation of the trend, since markets require new participants to continue. This is true of futures markets where the trend is heightened by those who are looking for a reversal of the underlying trend. The relationship of open interest to prices can be seen in the following SPI chart (Figure 15.6, opposite).

FIGURE 15.6 **SPI**

From this chart we are able to formulate a few rules for using open interest as a trading tool:

- Open interest acts as confirmation of a trend. Rising open interest during a decline in prices provides a rationale for adding to short positions since prices are likely to track lower as panicked bulls attempt to sell their positions. The same broad rule applies to uptrends. Rising open interest during price lifts is evidence of the involvement of bears who will have to buy back their positions to cover. Therefore traders would add to their long positions.

- If open interest falls during a rise in prices, it demonstrates that the trend is nearing maturity as bulls are taking any profits they can on positions and withdrawing. Likewise bears are covering their short positions. It is a common maxim in futures markets that the future is discounted so a fall in open interest during price rises is a sign of a possible reversal in trend.

- If open interest falls during a fall in prices it shows that the bears are covering their short positions and withdrawing. At the same time the bulls are still bottom-fishing. Traders should prepare for a reversal.

- When the levels of open interest plateau during a trend it shows that the trend is mature and that the most profitable trading periods have passed. Prices are likely to flatten out in conjunction with open interest.

16 SENTIMENT-BASED OSCILLATORS

To DATE WE HAVE examined price action in its rawest form. However, for many traders such analysis is often felt to be inadequate in offering sufficient comfort to pull the trigger. As such most traders look to sentiment-based oscillators to offer them sufficient weight of evidence to commit to a trade.

Sentiment-based oscillators are based upon the presumption that markets move on sentiment. As such traders need a variety of indicators to highlight and analyse this sentiment. In essence they need to know who is in the driver's seat, the bulls or the bears. Perhaps, more importantly, they need to know when a change in who is in charge might occur.

The interpretation of sentiment-based oscillators takes two forms. Firstly they are used to confirm the trend. Secondly they are used to highlight divergences between price and sentiment. Using them as trend confirmation is by far the simplest way to use them. It is also a very unsophisticated approach. This approach revolves around an acknowledgement of what the trend is and then confirming that by looking at an oscillator.

The real power of oscillators, should you choose to use them, is to be found in their power to highlight dislocations between price and sentiment. I will examine divergences in more depth at the end of this chapter.

169

Momentum

Momentum essentially measures the rate of change of prices. It is the market's speedometer. Momentum tells us how sustainable trends are. We are measuring the change in the way the herd is feeling; how optimistic or how pessimistic investors are. It is a leading indicator in that extremes in momentum occur before extremes in the underlying price. It can also function as a parallel indicator.

Momentum has a positive and negative scale. As you would expect, a positive momentum indicates that the mood of traders is buoyant; a negative momentum indicates that traders are pessimistic. However, this is only half the story. Momentum trends like all other indicators, and it is the direction of the trend that is most important to us. As momentum peaks ahead of price action we know that the current mood in the market is unsustainable, and either a reversal or slowing in the trend is on the horizon. It is this part of the analysis we have to be careful with. For example, if momentum has been positive and begins to slip, it is not a given that the trend will reverse. As can be seen in the example below, it is possible for momentum to slow without the underlying trend breaking. Still, such a situation is not without opportunities. Consider the example of Optus (CWO) in Figure 16.1.

FIGURE 16.1 **CWO** WITH MOMENTUM

Momentum has several facets that need to be explored. In this example, a rising momentum indicates that the underlying trend is accelerating and that it is likely to continue. When momentum slips to a lower peak, it shows that the trend is slowing—its acceleration is slowing. In such a situation it is best to think of a car that is rolling after the engine has been switched off. Markets can continue moving on inertia for some time. Such a development is a warning sign that the underlying trend may have run out of puff. To return to our car analogy, it will roll as long as it has sufficient energy but it will stop unless the engine is turned back on. The market is the same—it will coast, but eventually the underlying trend will come to an end if new buyers do not enter the market.

In examining the peaks of momentum it is necessary to understand that because momentum is a relative indicator we are literally seeing how traders felt yesterday compared with today. As momentum ran up in February, the mood of traders was buoyant and optimism was growing. This can be seen by the underlying trend, which has also moved up. However, notice in early March momentum began to trace lower tops. In essence it was trending down whilst price was still trying to move higher. This bearish divergence was a sign that an interim top was nearby. The optimism of traders was shrinking, yet prices continued to move higher. Such a situation is unsustainable, and prices began to track lower in April.

Notice, however, that we have to be cognisant of the underlying trend. Momentum can slip lower but not reverse prices. In early 2000, momentum began to slip but prices moved ahead. This is not to say that we should ignore a change in the trend of momentum but rather we should wait for confirmation before committing ourselves to the other side of the trend.

Positive confirmation of a change in trend comes when momentum drops through the horizontal axis as prices decline. A drop into negative territory is a strong signal that the mood of traders has actively slipped from optimistic to pessimistic.

The same rules that apply to positive momentum apply to negative momentum. When momentum traces a series of lower lows in conjunction with price it is safe to be a seller of whatever instrument we are trading.

Divergences between negative momentum and price can also warn traders to beware of a possible change in market sentiment, as in the following example of Coca-Cola Amatil (CCL—Figure 16.2, overleaf). In this instance price has moved to a new low but momentum has failed to confirm this move. This is a bullish divergence. Once again, all we are doing is sticking our head out of the window to have at look at the weather. It is unsophisticated and does not tell the future; all it tells us to do is pack an umbrella because we might need it.

FIGURE 16.2 **CCL** WITH MOMENTUM

COCA-COLA AMATIL-Daily 02/28/2001 C=5.180 .000 O=5.100 H=5.180 L=5.010 V=3480903

Falling price

Momentum 0.42

Rising momentum

2000   Feb   Mar   Apr   May

Created with SuperCharts by Omega Research © 1997

Momentum can function as either a leading or parallel indicator. Leading signals are given when momentum and price diverge. Rising price and falling momentum is a bearish divergence and when this occurs traders should lock-in upside profits and be ready for a possible change in trend. Falling prices and rising momentum is a bullish divergence; traders should lock-in downside profits and get ready for a possible change in trend.

When prices and momentum move in concert it is safe to trade aggressively in the direction of the trend. If price and momentum are rising, this is bullish. If price and momentum are falling this is bearish.

When momentum swings from either positive to negative or negative to positive then this is a strong signal to watch the prevailing trend and to trade the change in sentiment aggressively. A swing through the horizontal is a signal that traders should have prepared for when divergences between momentum and price were first noticed.

Stochastic Indicator

The stochastic indicator is based on the premise that closing prices tend to accumulate at the top of a trading range during an uptrend and at the bottom of a trading range during a downtrend. What you are seeing when you view a stochastic indicator is the momentum or power of each of the market's participants to close the market at a point that they are comfortable with. Bulls would like to see the market close at its highs whereas the bears would like to close it at its lows. The stochastic indicator measures the relationship between high, low and close—and hence the power of bulls and bears—on a scale of 1 to 100.

When plotting stochastics we are generally faced with a choice between two indicator types: a fast stochastic and a slow stochastic. The fast stochastic is extremely sensitive to changes in the market. It has a tendency to produce too many false breaks because of its sensitivity. The fast stochastic can be seen in Figure 16.3.

FIGURE 16.3   DOW JONES WITH FAST STOCHASTIC

Many traders are drawn to any indicator with the word fast in front of it, much as they believe that if they use a moving average of very short duration then they will get every swing in the market. Many male traders are drawn to it because they consider themselves aggressive and manly and it is only befitting that such a trader use a very aggressive tool to engage the market. These are rather naive and childish assumptions.

The slow stochastic in Figure 16.4 (overleaf) is less sensitive and produces a smoother, more trending curve. This approach produces fewer false breakouts and gives a clearer signal during times of strong price action. It is the slow stochastic and its interpretation that I will concentrate on.

FIGURE 16.4 AUSTRALIAN DOLLAR WITH SLOW STOCHASTIC

As can be seen from this chart there are a variety of signals that can be generated by the stochastic indicator. Traditionally it is regarded that the stochastic serves as an overbought/oversold indicator. When the indicator moves out of its trading range to beyond the upper or lower reference line then the underlying instrument is overbought or oversold. However, note the predominant trend for the $A during the period of study. The $A is firmly ensconced in a down move. During this phase the stochastic moved beyond the lower reference line on four occasions. Such a move may have convinced the novice that the $A was oversold and due to reverse. The reversals that did take place were only small counter-trend reversals that would only have benefited the most aggressive trader. Worse, they may have tempted the novice to go long in the face of a prolonged bear phase.

Expressions such as overbought and oversold need to be treated with a great deal of scepticism since they are relative terms that only hold meaning during the period of the stochastic. For example the $A may have been oversold during the time period of the oscillator, which in this instance was 15 days. The only way a judgement such as overbought or oversold can be made with any degree of certainty is with the benefit of hindsight.

To further illustrate the difficulty of spotting overbought and oversold zones consider Figure 16.5 (opposite).

FIGURE 16.5 OPTISCAN WITH SLOW STOCHASTIC

During early 2001 Optiscan (OIL) moved down strongly but the stochastic only barely made it into overbought territory before reversing its trend. If you had been waiting for a move into overbought territory before initiating any form of stop loss you would have been too late.

In October OIL moved into overbought territory. If you had sold here because of a value judgement you would have missed the final part of the uptrend. The stochastic can either slip just into overbought or oversold before reversing, thereby catching the slow trader unawares, or it can move into overbought or oversold and hold there for some time whilst the underlying trend continues to move price. It is because of this fuzziness that traders should be very wary about making exit or entry judgements based upon the stochastic.

In a bull market the stochastic can spend several months above the reference line in what is typically referred to as being overbought before any slackening in the upward price of the underlying instrument is seen. Likewise in a bear market, a stochastic can give a reading of oversold for many months before prices begin to reverse their trend and move back up.

> *"It is because of this fuzziness that traders should be very wary about making exit or entry judgements based upon the stochastic."*

Scale

This brings us to an important point that is always overlooked by traders and authors alike. A stochastic scale has no relationship to the price action of the underlying instrument. I have lost count of the number of times I have heard traders lament the fact that a stochastic has moved from 20 to 70 but the stock or index has only moved a few points. The stochastic is essentially a dimension-less indicator. We are not really interested in its scale but rather its direction. It is impossible to compare the scale of the stochastic with the price of a stock and expect there to be some relationship between the two. I have seen the stochastic move through its entire range and back whilst the stock I have been trading has moved only a few cents.

In interpreting the stochastic we require a good degree of intuition and finesse. It is one of those times in trading where science gives way to art and common sense.

Trends

Always trade in the direction of the trend of the stochastic, not against it. The stochastic can remain overbought or oversold for some time before the price action begins to reflect any slowing in the prevailing trend.

If you see a divergence between the price and the oscillator, wait for the price action to falter and for the stochastic to move away from the reference line before initiating a trade. Trading signals generated by divergences must include the following caveat; they are at their most effective when the stochastic shows a series of reversals before crossing the reference line. If the stochastic reverses below the reference line whilst prices continue to rise this is a bearish divergence. If the stochastic reverses above the reference line whilst prices continue to fall this is a bullish divergence.

If the stochastic is moving in the opposite direction to the underlying trend it means that the market is churning. If the stochastic breaks through the reference line, yet the market remains ensconced in its trend, it means that the market will slow. This is often the prelude to a change in trend. If nothing else, this sort of divergence acts as a brake on the prevailing trend in that it shows that the dominant market group may be faltering. However, such an interpretation is not set in stone. You must be flexible in your interpretation of the stochastic.

Shape

Watch the shape of the stochastic curve. A great deal of information can be distilled from the shape. In an uptrend, if the peak of the stochastic beyond the upper reference line is narrow and sharply defined it means that the bulls are weak and the market may suffer a sharp reversal. If the stochastic has a very broad top then it indicates the power of the bulls to close prices at the high of the day is undiminished and any decline may be short lived. However, a broad top can only exist for so long before the bulls fatigue, and a pullback after an extended top is likely to be spectacular. Traders should wait for the stochastic to drop below the reference line and for the underlying trend to weaken before going short. In downtrends a narrow wedge-shaped base below the reference line indicates that the bears are weak and the market is likely to bounce. A broad base indicates that the bears hold sway and it may be some time before prices recover.

Relative Strength Index (RSI)

If there is an analytical technique that causes confusion by virtue of its very name then it is the RSI. The RSI is a measure of momentum; it is not a comparison between two separate stocks or commodities. When we measure the RSI we are measuring whether a move is accelerating or decelerating, we are not trying to define whether BHP is stronger than the All Ordinaries Index.

Once again the RSI is traditionally plotted with reference lines and these are used to make some form of determination as to whether the underlying instrument is overbought or oversold. Such a traditional interpretation can be seen in Figure 16.6.

FIGURE 16.6   GOLD WITH RSI

As gold moves towards the upper reference line it is considered to be overbought. When it approaches the lower reference line it is considered to be oversold. This is the traditional mechanism for interpreting the RSI. There is a subset of this interpretation in that it is believed that the trend and the RSI should move in the same direction, thereby providing a degree of comfort for the trader.

However I would like to suggest an alternative interpretation since I believe that the power of oscillators in helping traders pull the trigger lies in their ability to spot divergences and thereby provide traders with a degree of psychological comfort regarding their decision. The previous method of plotting the RSI makes it difficult to spot divergences of any type. My suggestion is to overlay the RSI on a line chart and then attempt to make an interpretation, as shown below.

FIGURE 16.7 CWO WITH RSI OVERLAY

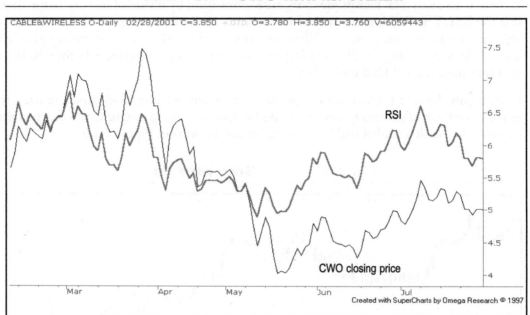

> *"My suggestion is to overlay the RSI on a line chart...this allows for a much easier interpretation of divergences."*

Plotting the RSI in this manner allows for a much easier interpretation of divergences. As can be seen from this chart of Optus (CWO) the period March to April saw an acceleration in the share price. Simultaneously the RSI, instead of making new highs, made a lower high.

Such a formation is known as a Type 1 bearish divergence (see Figure 16.8, opposite). In such a formation price moves to a new high whereas the oscillator moves to a lower high. As you would expect the reverse of the Type 1 bearish divergence is the Type 1 bullish divergence. In this formation price moves to a new low but the oscillator moves to a shallower low.

FIGURE 16.8 CWO WITH RSI OVERLAY

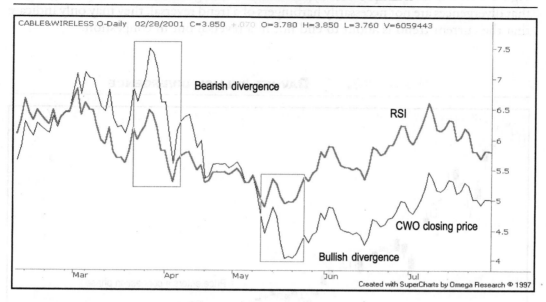

It is possible for divergences to occur in any oscillator. Figure 16.9 is an example of a Type 1 bearish divergence using the MACD histogram. Prices moved to a new high whereas the histogram made lower and lower peaks.

FIGURE 16.9 DAVNET MACD BEARISH DIVERGENCE

Figure 16.10 is an example of a Type 1 bullish divergence. This example highlights that divergences are not necessarily harbingers of a trend reversal, they may only indicate that the current trend is about to end not in a reversal but in congestion.

FIGURE 16.10   DAVNET BULLISH DIVERGENCE

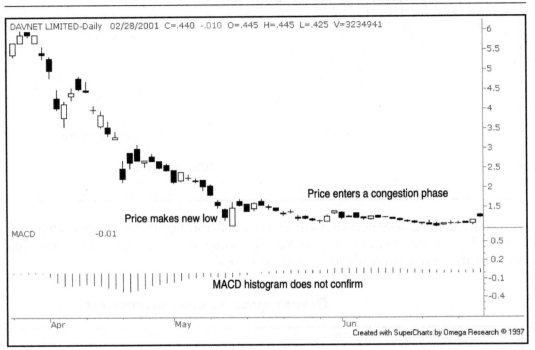

Divergences

There are three types of divergences that are thought to occur in markets. We have already discussed the Type 1 divergences. As you would expect the others are known as Type 2 and Type 3 divergences—technical analysts are nothing if not imaginative in their naming of things. I will only consider the Type 2 divergences, since the Type 3 are so rare as to almost never occur.

In a Type 2 bullish divergence price makes a double bottom and the oscillator makes a shallower low. The double bottom when considered in isolation is the true buy signal since it is generated purely by price action. The oscillator merely adds confirmation to the initial signal.

An example of such a signal can be seen in Figure 16.11 (opposite).

FIGURE 16.11 WESTPAC OSCILLATOR BULLISH DIVERGENCE

Westpac (WBC) tries to make a new low but price merely forms a base. The MACD histogram makes a shallower low. Note in this instance WBC actually made a triple bottom (notice the two candles in the second low). What such a formation shows is the unwillingness of traders to push prices below this point. Their reasoning may be because of perceived notions of value at this point, or a change in the macro features surrounding WBC and other banks. The thinking behind this decision of the crowd not to push prices lower is largely irrelevant. What matters is that price is offering a trading signal which is clean and should not be complicated by the need to over-analyse the stock.

> *"The thinking behind this decision of the crowd is ...largely irrelevant. What matters is that price is offering a trading signal which is clean..."*

As would be expected a Type 2 bearish divergence occurs when price makes a double top and the oscillator makes a lower high.

In the example on the following page (Figure 16.12) the driving force behind the down-move is the reluctance of traders to push the price beyond $13.00. The divergence is merely confirmation of this reluctance.

FIGURE 16.12 WESTPAC OSCILLATOR BEARISH DIVERGENCE

Divergence Summary

Type 1 bullish: Price reaches a new low but the oscillator tracks to a shallower low.

Type 1 bearish: Price reaches a new high but the oscillator tracks to a lower high.

Type 2 bullish: Price makes a double bottom and the oscillator tracks to a shallower low.

Type 2 bearish: Price makes a double top and the oscillator makes a lower high.

Divergences can occur between price and any oscillator over any timeframe. However I need to introduce a note of caution: divergences are a rare phenomenon. They do not occur once a week. Powerful divergences may only occur a few times every year so to spend your life looking for divergences is simply a waste of time. If you are diligent about looking at price then when divergences occur they will be obvious to you.

The same warning that I give about every technical indicator also applies to divergences. They are not the Holy Grail. They will not guarantee you success. The only thing that guarantees survival and in turn guarantees success is risk management.

As with the stochastic indicator the RSI requires traders to be flexible in their interpretation of the signals that are generated. Once again the strength and direction of the prevailing trend should be uppermost in our mind when we view the RSI. For example a reading of +80 would normally be considered overbought with the instrument we are measuring ready to reverse. However in a bull market such a reading may be quite common and stocks may hold this level for some time before reversing.

Traders cannot be too dogmatic in their approach to deciphering sentiment-based indicators. Each commodity has to be viewed in its own historical context. However, the hard and fast rule is that if a commodity is above 80 then it is overbought, if it is below 20 it is oversold. The problem with this inflexible approach is that many commodities do not hit these magic marks, so our RSI has to be redesigned to take into account how a particular commodity actually performs rather than how we think it should perform. Most software packages will allow you to alter the settings on the scale of an RSI chart so that you can base your interpretation on reality. For example, consider the following chart.

FIGURE 16.13   GOLD WITH RSI

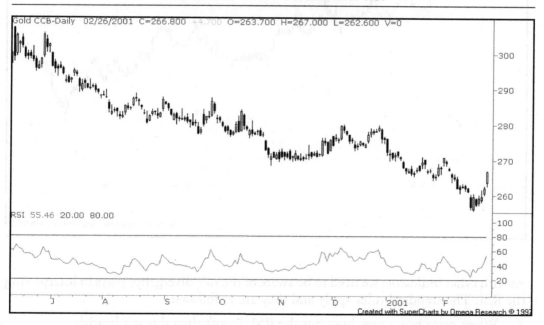

This chart shows that gold almost never moved above 80 or below 20. Conventional wisdom would have dictated that we only consider the stock to fulfil our overbought or oversold criteria if it had moved into these zones. As a consequence our analysis would have been skewed by our misunderstanding of the role historical data plays in the interpretation of the RSI.

Consider the chart in Figure 16.14. In this chart I have altered the values that define overbought and oversold to reflect reality. Notice that the correlation between price reversals and the new levels is now much stronger. This example of gold, which has been in a downtrend for years, is a good illustration of how the trader must be aware of the power of the underlying trend. Any moves in price away from being overbought were sharp and an extension of the underlying trend. Any moves from being oversold were sluggish and offered no real trading opportunities.

FIGURE 16.14   GOLD WITH REVISED RSI

As with other indicators we need to be aware of the role divergence plays in interpreting the RSI. The standard rules apply and they are as follows:

1. When price hits a new high but the RSI doesn't then this is a bearish divergence. The importance of this signal is intensified if the first peak in the RSI is above the reference line but the second is not.

2. When price hits a new low but the RSI doesn't then this is a bullish divergence. The signal has added weight if the RSI hits its first low below the reference line and the second low above the reference line.

The RSI displays traditional charting patterns like double tops/bottoms and head and shoulders. Traders should act upon these in the same manner as they would as if they had occurred in the underlying commodity.

Price action should be watched carefully when the RSI drifts beyond its reference lines. As I said earlier these reference lines should reflect the historical trading patterns of the stock. It should not be automatically assumed that a given commodity is overbought or oversold because it has gone beyond its reference lines.

Divergence patterns are important in interpreting the RSI. Traders should be familiar with both bullish and bearish divergences.

Part V

GETTING STARTED

"What the hell do you do all day?"

My father on innumerable occasions

17 THE TRADER'S BUSINESS PLAN

TRADING IS PERHAPS BEST DESCRIBED as a very dynamic, fluid game of strategy. As such it requires the trader to have a plan to engage the market. Many novice traders believe that trading is a spontaneous, disorganised environment. Males perceive it to be a testosterone-charged arena whereby they are locked in mortal combat with the market. Unfortunately for the trader who is looking for boundless excitement akin to what would be found in a casino this is not true.

Trading requires a structure. In essence the trader brings order to chaos. It is at this part of the trading journey that most traders fail—traders need rules and the rules need to be adhered to. This is one of the prime maxims of trading—no rules, no profit. It is simple, like most things to do with trading.

The generation of and adherence to rules is extremely difficulty for traders. Part of the difficulty lies in the need for the rules to be self-generated. Through life individuals are told what to do. All the rules that are encountered are generated by others. As a child it is parental rules that set boundaries, at school it is the structure of the school that dictates behaviour. As an adult rules are imposed by society, the hours that are worked are dictated by the employer, behaviour is defined as acceptable or unacceptable, even the road rules are strictly codified—as they should be. All of these rules leave little room for interpretation and more importantly they are imposed from an external source. Trading is not like this.

In trading all the rules of conduct are generated by the individual. Traders have to set their own rules and these govern how a trade is entered, when it is exited and how much risk is absorbed. Neither the exchange nor a broker provide any rules for trading. They might provide rules of business conduct but these are not rules to trade by. It is at this point that the trading process begins to break down. Most individuals have no concept of generating their own rules of conduct. As such it is impossible for most to formulate rules that can be applied to trading since they have no experience at self-determination and, even more importantly, self-discipline.

The concepts of self-determination and self-discipline are central to a trader's life—they cannot be emphasised enough. A trader without these attributes will fail, and there is a fairly simple test that can determine whether a novice trader will be sufficiently self-disciplined enough to enjoy longevity in the markets. If you are a novice trader and are wondering whether you have what it takes, try this. Get up at 4.30 a.m. every morning for the next two weeks. That's it.

Whilst this test does suffer from being externally imposed it still requires self-discipline. It is a test, and it will point out to you very early in your trading career the sort of person you are. If you fail this test you do not have what it takes to trade successfully over the long term.

It should also be noted that a trader's business plan is not a series of statements designed to get into a trade. That is a trigger. The rules for your trigger are buried within the rules of your trading plan. The business plan is a philosophical mission statement. If you cannot answer these questions then you have no idea as to what you want from the markets. If you do not know what you want then you do not know how to go about achieving your goals.

RULES FOR ASSEMBLING A BUSINESS PLAN

Philosophical Points

Why do you Want to be a Trader?

This is central to being a trader. This is the first point that should appear in your business plan. If you are attracted to the romance of trading or the belief that it is a get-rich-quick scheme then the markets are the wrong place for you.

Most people who attempt to trade markets fail, so the question needs to be asked: why do you want to engage in an activity where the majority fail? I am aware that everyone suffers from the myth of individual specialness, the belief that somehow each of us is special and somehow immune from the statistical statements that rule the world.

If I make the statement that eight out of ten individuals who attempt to trade fail, then 80% of all people who read this and then attempt to trade the markets will fail. As the old recruiting poster says: this means you!

This is in effect a two-part question: the second part pertains to what edge you will have in trading. You will need an edge in trading. If 80% of people fail as traders what makes you smarter, sharper, more intuitive or more disciplined than those who fail? The answer to this question will be your edge. If you do not know what your edge is then you do not have one. If you don't have one then don't trade.

What do you Think Being a Trader will Bring You?

Do you think trading will bring easy money, endless wealth, a racy lifestyle? If so then you are mistaken and you have prepared yourself already for failure. The great traders of the world trade for the sake of trading, money is a mere by-product of what they do. They are like athletes who compete for the sheer joy of competing. Merely changing your income will not change your life.

What are you Willing to Risk to Achieve Your Goal?

Many make the mistake of believing this is a monetary question—it is not. It is a question of personal commitment. Trading is hard work. Let no one tell you otherwise. It takes time, effort and dedication, and along the way there will be many failures. All of these will take their toll on you and those around you, so you will need to be firmly committed to the goal of becoming a trader.

There is a wider question here and it pertains to success and the attitudes that surround it. The majority of individuals are not very good at success. Self-sabotage is a common human trait. The reasons for this are many and varied and are often buried deep within the psyche, and I have touched upon them in the discussion on the psychology of trading, but I will revisit one of these reasons since it is relevant to the novice. Success brings change, change brings tension. It also brings conflict with long-held values such as the old-fashioned work ethic. Trading has the allure of easy money and many times it will appear as if the rewards it brings have not been earned. This conflicts with many internal belief systems and a cycle of self-sabotage is engaged.

> *"The great traders of the world trade for the sake of trading, money is a mere by-product of what they do."*

There is also a time component in this; trading takes time. If you are not willing to put in the time then you will not succeed.

Trade to Survive

Do not worry about making money. If you survive you will make more money than you ever imagined possible. If you don't survive then you won't make any money at all.

Plan for the Worst-Case Scenario

Every trader should be emotionally prepared for the absolute worst-case scenario. This should be addressed in building your trading system, but you should also prepare for it mentally. It has been estimated that the chance of a severe price shock occurring during a trading career is as high as 10%. Practise how you would react to an event such as the one shown below.

FIGURE 17.1   BIOTA

This is not an aberration in the chart, it is the actual course of trade in Biota. Traders would have gone to bed safe in the knowledge that Biota was holding onto the $9.00 level only to wake up the next morning and see the stock open at $5.00, before eventually bouncing off an intraday low of $3.00. How would you have handled such stress?

Practical Considerations

What Timeframe are you Going to Trade?

Many traders enter the markets with dreams of being intraday traders. They are drawn to what they perceive to be the excitement of the trading floor and the lure of easy money. Surely all you need to do to be a successful intraday trader is to buy at the low and sell at the high for the day. How hard can that be? It is here that another dose of reality is needed. Long-term studies have shown that 95% of all day traders make no money. Novice traders enter trading with little or no skill and expect to trade the most dynamic and chaotic of timeframes.

It is possible for traders to engage the market over multiple timeframes but these timeframes and the rules for engagement must be clearly stated before beginning

What Markets are you Going to Trade?

This question relates to location and market type. If you wish to trade overseas markets then you must be prepared for trading overnight since this is when overseas markets are open. It is also important to note that when trading foreign markets three trading decisions are made; country, currency and then company. The trader who engages foreign markets is also trading the currency and the country so the trader will need to have a view of these features, not just the individual stock.

There is also the question of whether you will trade shares, options, warrants or futures. Be warned if you cannot trade shares successfully and be consistently profitable over the longer term then you will not be able to trade highly-leveraged derivatives. Whilst many novice traders have dreams about being highly-successful commodity traders the chances of success are limited. A recent straw poll I saw conducted among futures advisers indicated that of every 200 new clients that come to them only one or two survive more than a few months.

If you cannot drive, then you cannot drive—it does not matter what type of car you buy.

Irrespective of the market you decide to trade it must have sufficient liquidity to allow you to trade with the knowledge that you will be able to get out. Many sharemarkets contain instruments that simply lack sufficient liquidity to trade. A trading methodology should contain a means of measuring liquidity. This problem also applies to certain overseas futures markets that have trading limits. These markets, in the event of a large move in any given direction, close to trading, thereby locking the trader into a position that cannot be exited until the move has peaked, thus guaranteeing a large loss.

The Holy Grail is a Myth

A trader's business plan is not a road map in search of the Holy Grail, that one mystical tool that will slay the demons of the market and make a trader endlessly profitable. The Grail is a fairytale along with Santa Claus and the Easter Bunny. A business plan should not contain any reference to any of them.

Unsuccessful traders continually seek out a magic indicator. They scour the Internet, they buy every new software package they can find, they even go as far as joining little clubs whose members are of the same ilk in the vain hope that someone might know the secret of trading.

When it comes to implementing the system you have designed be aware of its shortcomings, but if it feels comfortable to you then this is your system. Stick to it. Do not look for the Holy Grail.

The Lone Gunman

The majority of individuals are social and by nature humans are herd animals. This presents tremendous challenges for the trader. There is a desperate human need for contact and validation. This is why novice traders often join share trading groups. These groups offer emotional support but little else of value. Unfortunately having a trading partner or being the member of a share trading group that seeks consensus as opposed to supporting the individual in trading decisions is a recipe for disaster. Share trading groups have appalling rates of return.

Having to rely upon someone else will ultimately compound the pressures of trading, eventually leading to conflict over decision-making. If you believe that someone else is a better trader than you then do not hinder their performance by being a millstone around their neck. Give them your money to trade on your behalf and go and do something you are going to enjoy.

Time Out

A plan should have a time-out clause in it to cope with the need for holidays, a build-up of stress or illness. Never trade when emotionally distracted or ill. The market will still be there when you come back.

Advice

In a prominent place in all trading environments should be the statement: never take advice from anyone. If brokers knew what they were talking about then they would not be talking to you. As was previously stated if someone is a superior trader to you then give them your money and do something else.

Trading System Design

There are three essential components to designing a trading system. They are:

1. A position-sizing algorithm
2. An exit trigger
3. An entry trigger.

Requirements for a Trading System

Look Down Not Up

Trading is an information management exercise. Too many traders believe that trading is like panning for gold and that if you pan for long enough you will find the one nugget that has eluded everybody else. As such they begin their quest by looking through every available stock. Well, consider this; in Australia there are approximately 1,200 listed shares. If you spend 15 minutes looking at each one then your analysis will take approximately 18,000 minutes, or 300 hours, or 12.5 days.

Traders should adopt a top-down approach as part of their trading system. This approach could take on a format similar to this:

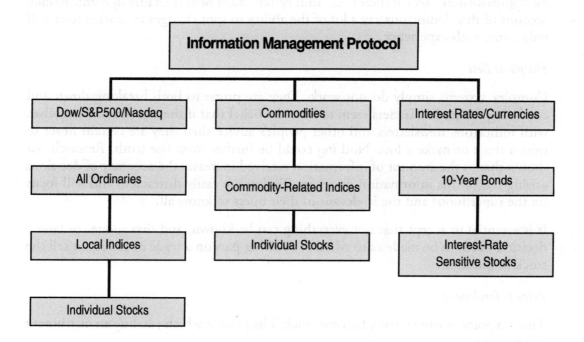

This protocol will require you to put in some effort so that you are aware of, for example, what are commodity-related stocks and how changes in interest rates and currencies impact upon stocks, or it may require you to build an index of technology-related stocks if you are interested in trading technology issues.

This is grunt work. It is boring and it is time consuming, but it must be done if the trading process is to be made simpler.

Part of this process may involve looking at longer-term indicators. This gives a backdrop to the current trading environment. This may include very broad models such as looking at overall market trends to gain an indication of market sentiment, or advance/decline lines to gauge market health.

Trend-Following

All trading systems must follow trends. It does not matter whether the market is engaged over very short or very long timeframes. The prevailing trend must be followed. There is no other way to make money in the market.

Robust

Market conditions change. It is estimated that prices only trend in a coherent fashion for approximately 20% of their lives. Your system must be sufficiently dynamic to take account of this. Unfortunately a lot of the ability to spot changes in market tone will only come with experience.

Simple is Best

Complex systems simply do not work. They are prone to both breaking down and confusing the trader. Traders seem to have the belief that if they surround themselves with indicators, newsletters and other people's advice then they are certain never to miss a trade or make a loss. Nothing could be further from the truth. Research has shown that as the amount of information received increases the accuracy of decisions arising out of this information decreases. Traders are easily distracted, and will focus on the superfluous and the irrelevant in their quest to know all.

It is essential to accept that not everything can be known, and that sooner or later a decision needs to be made as to whether to either pass on a trade or to buy or sell the stock in question.

Price is Irrelevant

This is a point at which many become stuck. The price at which you buy an instrument is irrelevant.

It is irrelevant for two reasons:

↪ Buying is not a very important decision, yet it is the decision traders spend the most time on. The price at which you buy an instrument has no bearing on whether in the long-term you are a profitable trader or not.

↪ The second reason why price is irrelevant is that it is prone to subjective interpretation. What you think to be expensive or cheap is irrelevant. Your opinion is worthless. The only opinion that counts is the market's opinion and the market will drive price in the direction it thinks to be most appropriate.

THE TRADING DECISION

HAVING LOOKED AT THE PSYCHOLOGY of trading, money management and basic indicators it is now time to review the trading decision. The decision to actually buy or sell an instrument is the easiest decision in trading and is the least important when it comes to determining whether you will be a profitable trader. The paradox in this is that, as we have seen, indicators take the most time to explain but they are the least important part of trading. Psychology and money management are the most important but take the least amount of time to explain. The actual trading decision is a similar paradox—the decision to trade actually takes some time as the trader waits for certain milestones or triggers to be engaged.

> *"The decision to actually buy or sell an instrument is the easiest decision in trading..."*

I want to review the trading decision by looking at a very simple technical trigger. This trigger will consist of a simple candlestick chart for viewing ease, an 18-day weighted moving average combined with volume and a MACD histogram whose default values are 12, 26 and 9.

Now before you go and write down these points as if they were some form of Holy Grail, they are not. They are simply the defaults that were in the program when I created the chart shown on the following page.

FIGURE 18.1 OPTISCAN

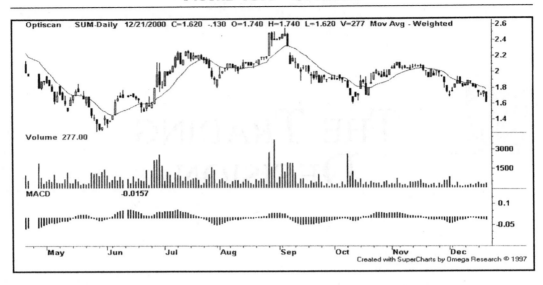

What the numbers are does not matter. It does not matter if the moving average is simple, weighted, exponential, sine-corrected or whatever. Nor does it really matter what time period it is. Why would 18 be better than 17 or 19? If you madly scribble down these parameters then you are giving away your status as a novice trader. Your trigger can be anything you choose. It really doesn't matter. All it needs to be is simple and consistent. However, I will demonstrate how an effective system can be built around this entry trigger.

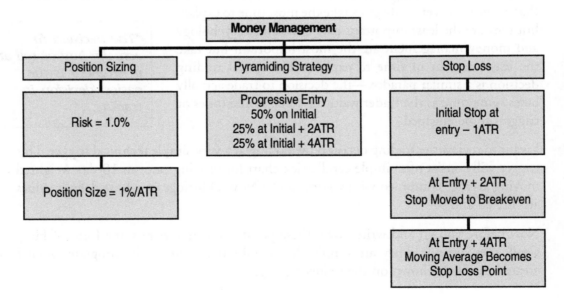

Notice the first step in the trade is not to try and find a perfect entry, it is to decide on an acceptable level of risk, what points will be used to add to a position and where stops will be placed to ensure a clean exit.

The second stage in trade initiation becomes one of trade selection. Trade selection is not a matter of merely buying whatever your broker or taxi driver told you to buy. It actually requires some work on your part. Much of this work is also done before actually trading.

It is important to have some idea of how the world works before even contemplating trading. My approach to trading is based upon an understanding of the big picture (see below). All things are interrelated, with the direction of our market largely being dictated by the direction of the US markets. For brief periods of time the markets may uncouple but this is more often than not an artifact produced by the weighting of components within the All Ordinaries Index.

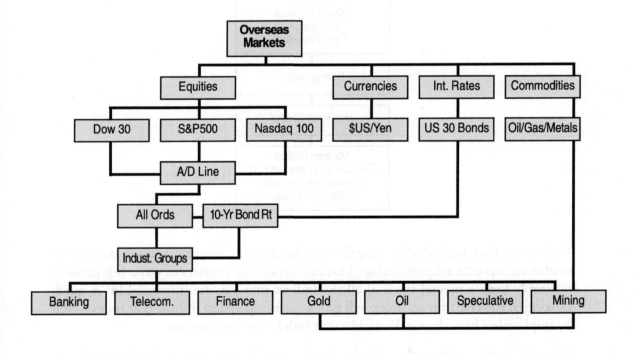

The All Ordinaries is a weighted index. As such some stocks exert a disproportionate influence on the market thereby giving the appearance that we are going our own way. As I write this we have experienced such a market phase; the All Ordinaries has hit an all-time high whereas the Dow is steadfastly ensconced in a sideways trend. The reason for this is News Corp. exerting its influence on the Index. At the time of writing the majority of stocks in Australia are going sideways, as they are in the US. This is why it is necessary to look in more depth at markets. Merely making a judgement by taking a cursory glance at the relevant index is simply not sufficient. It is necessary to examine the relevant advance/decline lines, which give an indication of the true health of a market.

Notice how the trading decision involves a top-down approach. To illustrate how this would work, consider an example involving the rise in the price of oil. The first step is to recognise that the price of oil has actually increased. This is done by viewing a chart of the oil price, either from a direct data provider or from a source such as Bloomberg.com or Quote.com. The next step is to view the energy index. If this is trending up then view the individual stocks within the index.

This can be summarised as:

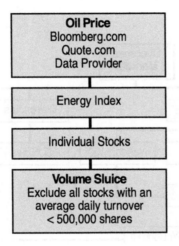

Notice how that, instead of looking for individual stocks, the first decision is to isolate market sectors that are performing. This can be done in a variety of ways. It is possible to simply keep a mental track of all the indices that you are interested in. A quick viewing of the chart for an index will give a clear impression of how that index—and by implication how the stocks within that index—are performing.

I have included a volume sluice in the decision-making tree because it is imperative to obey the liquidity rules that were set in the earlier parts of this book. I need to stress that the search for trading opportunities is not the search for a nugget that no one else has found. In trading it is imperative to be where there is activity. Trading is an auction. The only means traders have of competing is price—by definition an auction will be more competitive if there are multiple participants.

From this point it is a matter of selecting those shares that conform to the volume-based rules for inclusion. The next step is to apply the rules for the trigger to the shares selected. A possible trigger could include the following steps:

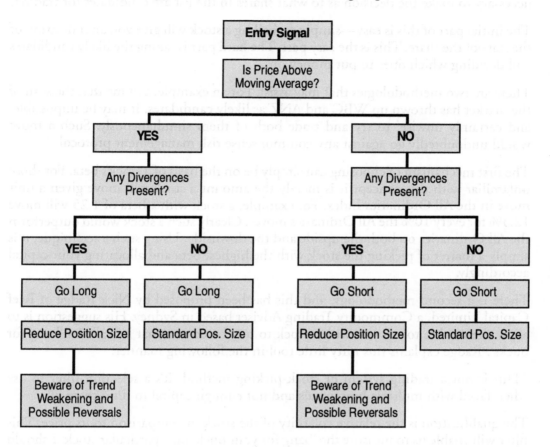

This is a very simple trigger, and is based purely upon a moving average and the isolation of divergences for spotting potential weaknesses in the prevailing trend. It is a simple trigger because it does not take account of any form of pattern recognition. It is purely trend-based.

It should be noted that this is only a trigger, it is not a trade management protocol. The trade management protocol was decided before the trade was engaged and included a form of risk analysis, when to pyramid into the position and when to exit the position.

The decision to enter a position can be based upon any coherent set of rules so long as they are uniform and consistent. The important phase of this analysis is to set the criteria regarding how much money you put into a stock, when this position will be added to and when to exit.

How to Select a Share

Having undergone whatever process is necessary to create a list of possibilities it is now necessary to make the decision as to what shares in the list are candidates for trading.

The initial part of this is easy—simply eyeballing a stock will give you an indication of the state of the share. This is the easy part. The hard part is taking the likely candidates and deciding which ones to put money on.

There are two methodologies that may assist. For an example, assume that the scan of the market has thrown up WBC and ANZ as likely candidates. It may be impossible, and certainly unwise, to try and trade both of them simultaneously. Such a move would undoubtedly go against any commonsense risk management protocol.

The first mechanism of choosing can simply be on the basis of a stock's beta. For those unfamiliar with this concept it is merely the amount a stock will move given a unit move in the All Ordinaries Index. For example, a stock with a beta of 1.25 will move 12.5% for every 10% the All Ordinaries moves. Clearly such a stock would outperform the All Ordinaries on both the upside and the downside. Using such a technique, it is simply a matter of picking the stock with the highest beta and allocating your capital accordingly.

There is a second methodology, and this has been proposed by Nick Radge of Reef Capital Limited, a Commodity Trading Adviser based in Sydney. His suggestion is to allow the market to tell you which stock to buy based on what he calls its 'bang for bucks'. Radge explains this nifty little tool in the following manner:

"This is not a trading system or stock-picking method. It's a selection filter to use when faced with multiple buy signals and not enough capital to fund them all.

The qualification is the relative volatility of the stock in comparison to its price. This filter will enable us to measure the 'bang for your buck' on a particular stock. I should point out that buying $10k worth of NAB is very different from buying $10k worth of NDP. You may get the NAB trade correct, but based on the capital used, the results will not be overly profitable. We need to get our monies worth and we need to make profits with the least amount of work.

$$[(10,000/Close) \times (Average\ Range,\ 200)]/100 = Possible\ dollar\ return$$

In layman's terms we divide a $10,000 account by the closing price on any given day. This number is then multiplied by the average range of the stock for the last 200 days. Dividing this number by 100 will convert the result to dollars and cents which in turn indicates the possible dollar return on any given day."

CANDLESTICK INTERPRETATION

by Louise Bedford, author of
The Secret of Candlestick Charting

What are Candlesticks?

Candlesticks utilise the same information as contained in a Western Bar Chart, however they look completely different. The thick part of the candle is called the *real body*. This shows the range between the opening and the closing price (see Figure 1). When the real body is white (or empty), it means that the close was higher than the opening price. When the real body is black (or filled in), the close was lower than the opening price.

FIGURE 1   CANDLESTICK

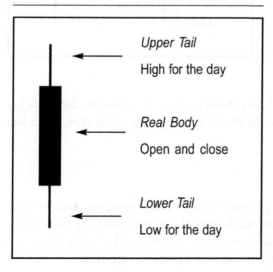

The thin lines above and below the real body are called the *wicks, tails* or *shadows* of the candle (regardless of on which side of the real body they are located). The upper tail (the high for the day on a daily chart) is located above the candlestick's real body, and the lower tail (the low for the day on a daily chart) is located below the real body. The tails are usually considered to be of less importance than the real body, as they represent extraneous price fluctuations. The open and the close are considered to be the most emotionally-charged points of the day and therefore they contain the highest level of significance in candlestick analysis.

The White Candle

The colour of the candle depicts whether the candle is bearish or bullish. When the day closes higher than it opened, this is a bullish sign. There is demand for the share and buyers are willing to pay higher and higher prices. The price is driven up as demand outstrips supply (see Figure 2).

The Black Candle

When the day closes lower than its opening price, it is a sign that sellers have fear in their hearts. This has the effect of driving the share price down. The market sentiment is pessimistic, creating a far greater supply of shares. Therefore the close is lower than the opening price, and the colour of the candle is black. A black candle clearly shows that the bears were in control for that period (see Figure 3).

FIGURE 2   WHITE CANDLE   FIGURE 3   BLACK CANDLE

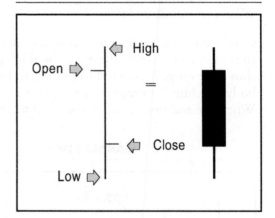

This tug of war between the bulls and the bears (buyers and sellers) forms the basis for each candlestick pattern formation. A single candlestick, or a group of candles, often has particular bullish or bearish significance.

When do we use Candlesticks?

Candlestick patterns fall into two broad groups; continuation patterns and reversal patterns. Continuation patterns suggest that the share will continue over the short-term in a particular direction. Reversal patterns mean that a share will change direction completely, or simply flatten into a sideways trend (see Figure 4, opposite).

FIGURE 4 REVERSAL AND CONTINUATION PATTERNS

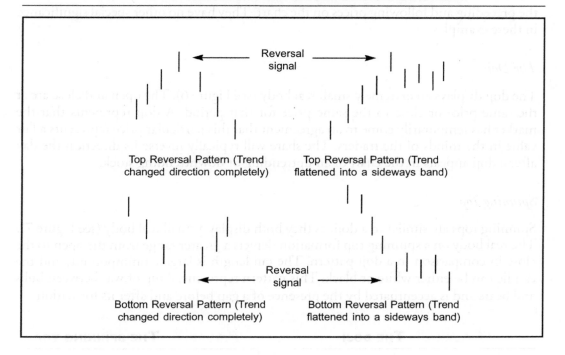

Reversal patterns are predictive if they occur once the share is trending, and will be the focus for the following discussion.

Common Candlestick Patterns

The Shooting Star

This pattern displays an upper tail length that is two times the length of the real body (see Figure 5). When a gap is present between the previous candle and the shooting star, the significance of this formation is intensified. This principle is relevant for all candlestick patterns. This pattern has greater significance if it is black. Shooting stars appear at the top of a trend and signify that the bears will be moving in with strength and that a downtrend is likely to occur.

FIGURE 5 SHOOTING STAR

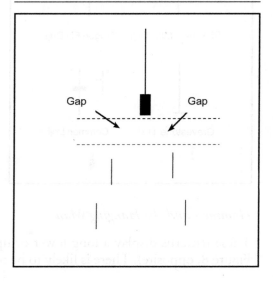

The small bars before and after the candlestick formation will show you the direction of the preceding and following prices on the chart. They have no other special significance in these examples.

The Doji

The doji displays an extremely small real body (see Figure 6). The open and close are at the same price or close to the same price for that period. A doji represents that the market has temporarily come to an agreement that this particular price represents a fair value in the minds of the traders. The share will typically reverse its direction the day after a doji appears in the chart of an uptrending or downtrending stock.

Spinning Top

Spinning tops are similar to a doji, as they both display a small real body (see Figure 7). The real body on a spinning top formation depicts a greater range from the open to the close in comparison to a doji pattern. The tail length is largely unimportant, and the candle can be either white or black. This pattern represents a tug of war between bulls and bears and is accentuated by the presence of a gap before and after its formation.

FIGURE 6 THE DOJI	FIGURE 7 THE SPINNING TOP

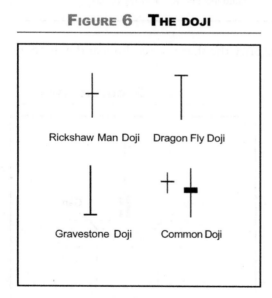

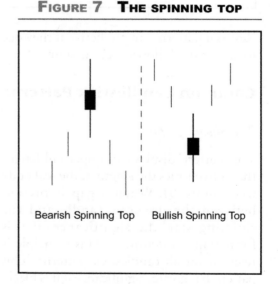

Hammers and the Hanging Man

These patterns display a long lower or upper tail above or below their real body (see Figure 8, opposite). There is likely to be no tail, or a very short tail on the other side of their real body. The tail length is required to be two times the length of the real body to fulfil the exact definition of this candle. Gaps increase the significance of the pattern. Look for these patterns at the top or bottom of trends to signify that a reversal is likely.

FIGURE 8   HAMMERS AND THE HANGING MAN

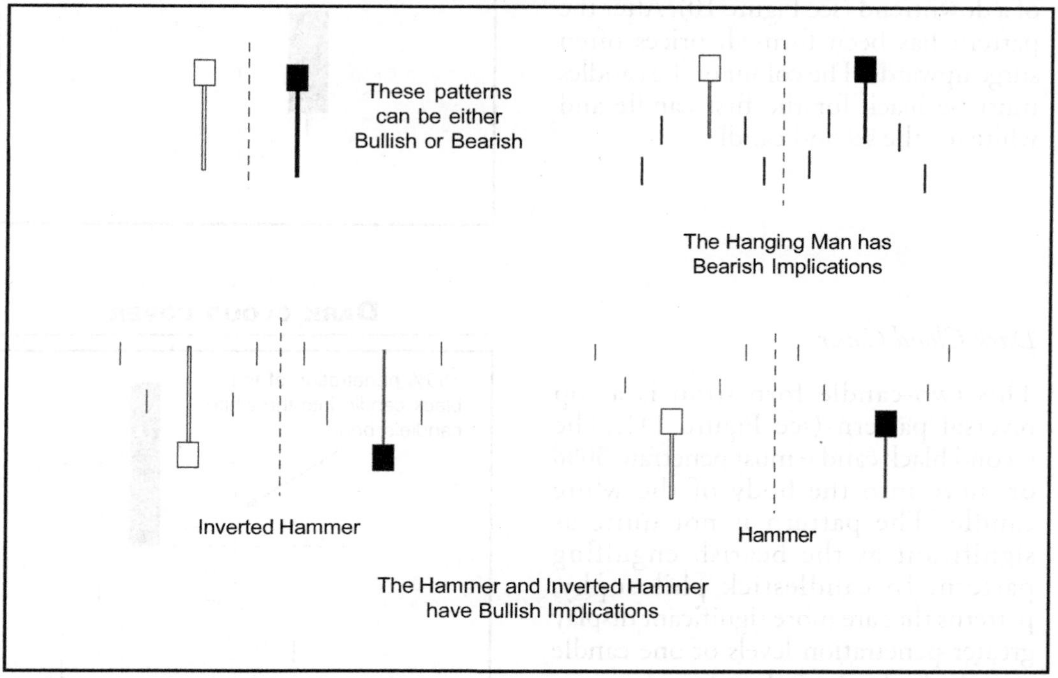

These patterns can be either Bullish or Bearish

The Hanging Man has Bearish Implications

Inverted Hammer

Hammer

The Hammer and Inverted Hammer have Bullish Implications

The Bearish Engulfing Pattern

This two-candle combination is an extremely effective pattern that often dramatically signifies the end of an uptrend (see Figure 9). After the appearance of this pattern, prices typically plunge downwards steeply. The second real body of this pattern totally engulfs the first real body and is a bearish sign as the price has closed lower than it opened for that period. The colour of the candles must be white for the first candle and black for the second candle.

FIGURE 9
BEARISH ENGULFING PATTERN

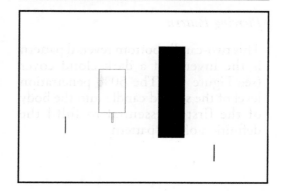

FIGURE 10
BULLISH ENGULFING PATTERN

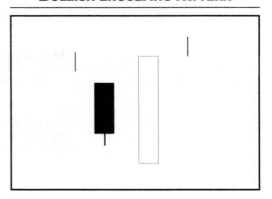

The Bullish Engulfing Pattern

This candle pattern often signifies the end of a downtrend (see Figure 10). After the pattern has been formed, prices often surge upwards. The colour of the candles must be black for the first candle and white for the second candle.

FIGURE 11
DARK CLOUD COVER

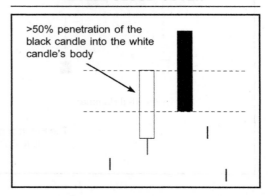

Dark Cloud Cover

This two-candle formation is a top reversal pattern (see Figure 11). The second black candle must penetrate 50% or more into the body of the white candle. The pattern is not quite as significant as the bearish engulfing pattern. In candlestick philosophy, patterns that are more significant display greater penetration levels of one candle into the body of another.

FIGURE 12
PIERCING PATTERN

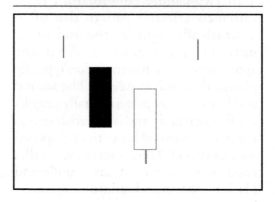

Piercing Pattern

This two-candle bottom reversal pattern is the inverse of a dark cloud cover (see Figure 12). The 50% penetration level of the second candle into the body of the first is essential to fulfil the definition of this pattern.

Evening Star

This bearish three-candle reversal pattern shows a long white real body (1), a small star of either colour (2), then a black real body (3) (see Figure 13). The evening star pattern is especially significant if there are gaps between each candle.

FIGURE 13 EVENING STAR

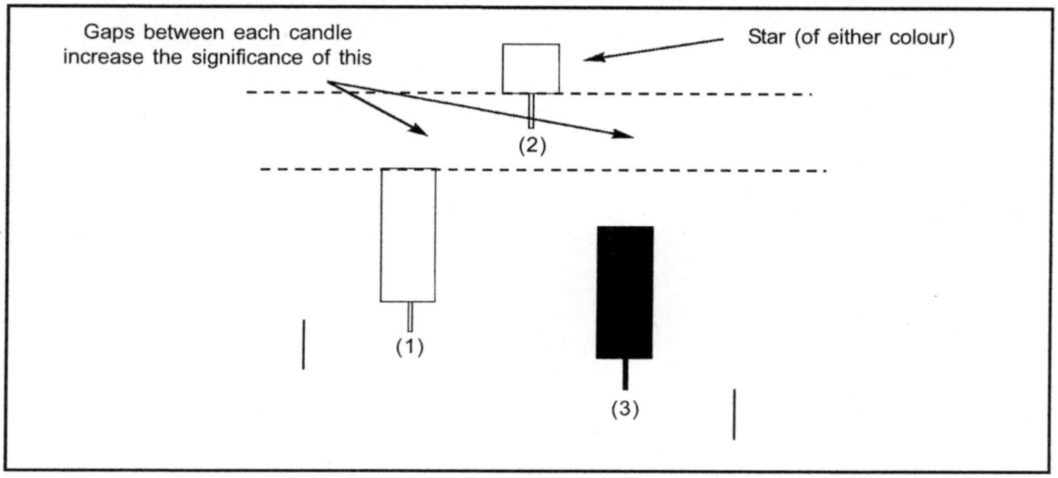

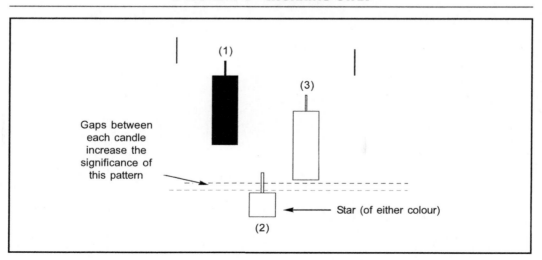

Morning Star

This bullish three-candle bottom reversal pattern shows a long black real body (1), a small star of either colour (2), then a white real body (3) (see Figure 14).

FIGURE 14 MORNING STAR

Louise Bedford is a full-time private trader and author. For a full discussion of the patterns described here and other relevant candlestick patterns refer to her books *The Secret of Candlestick Charting* and *The Secret of Writing Options* (both published by and available from Wrightbooks). For more information, you can also visit her website: www.tradingsecrets.com.au.

GLOSSARY

American option

An American option is an option that can be exercised at any point during its life.

At the market

An order to buy or sell a security at the prevailing market price. This is a quick and easy way to get into or out of the market. However there is a distinction between at market orders as done by a full-service broker and an at market order done by an online service. The full-service broker will execute the order at market either buying or selling all stock. An online service will merely take out the first line of the bid or offer and leave the remainder of the order at the last trade price.

At the money

An option is said to be at the money if the current market price is equal to the strike price.

Average down

Also known as dollar cost averaging, a strategy employed by amateurs and a guaranteed path to ruin.

Average True Range (ATR)

True range is the greatest of the following differences:

1. Today's high to today's low

2. Today's high to yesterday's close

3. Today's low to yesterday's close.

ATR is a measure of the range a stock may be expected to move during the day. The data has a period applied to it and is smoothed to produce a moving average of the ATR.

Back test

A mechanism whereby a system or indicator is tested for reliability using historical data.

Bar chart

Presentation of price data in a single bar comprising high, low, open, and close.

Bear/Bearish

A bear is someone with a negative view of either a market or an individual stock. The true origin of the expression is unclear but it is thought to have originated in the belief that bears claw back prices.

Beta

A measure of the volatility of a stock. Beta measures the movement of a given instrument relative to a benchmark such as a composite index. By definition the All Ordinaries Index will have a beta of one. If a stock has a beta of less than one then its move will be less than that of the All Ordinaries Index.

Bollinger bands

Bollinger bands plot trading bands above and below a simple moving average. The standard deviation of closing prices for a period equal to the moving average employed is used to determine the band width. This causes the bands to tighten in quiet markets and loosen in volatile markets. The bands can be used to determine overbought and oversold levels, locate reversal areas, project targets for market moves, and determine appropriate stop levels.

Dr Alexander Elder believes bands give the trader the ability to sell mania and buy fear. The strategy employed is to sell stocks as they move beyond the bands and buy stocks as price bounces from the lower levels.

The bands are used in conjunction with indicators such as RSI, MACD histogram, CCI and rate of change. Divergences between Bollinger bands and other indicators show potential reversal points.

Breakaway gap

An initial explosive move whereby prices open some distance from the previous close. Indicative of a rapid change in the underlying psychology of the market.

Breakeven point

The price at which a trader does not make or lose money.

Bull/Bullish

A trader who is bullish has an expectation that prices will rise.

Call option

A call option grants the option buyer the right but not the obligation to buy the underlying security at a set exercise or strike price on or before a given expiry date.

Candlestick charts

Method of drawing stock (or commodity) charts which originated in Japan.

Chaikin oscillator

The Chaikin oscillator is created by subtracting a 10-period exponential moving average of the Accumulation/Distribution line from a 3-period moving average of the Accumulation/Distribution Line.

Close out

The process of taking the opposite side of a transaction in order to remove any liability that may have arisen from the opening of an earlier position. If I had bought a futures contract I would close it out by selling the position.

Commodity Channel Index (CCI)

The CCI is a timing system that is best applied to commodity contracts which have cyclical or seasonal tendencies. The CCI does not determine the length of cycles—it is designed to detect when such cycles begin and end through the use of a statistical analysis which incorporates a moving average and a divisor reflecting both the possible and actual trading ranges. Although developed primarily for commodities, the CCI could conceivably be used to analyse stocks as well.

Commodity Selection Index

The Commodity Selection Index is related to the Directional Movement Index. Whereas the ADX (Average Directional Movement) plot of the DMI is used to rate contracts from the longer term, trend-following point of view, the CSI is used to rate items in the more volatile short term. The Commodity Selection Index takes into account the ADX from the Directional Movement Index, the Average True Range, the value of a one cent move as well as margin and commission requirements.

Confirmation

Traders look for three stages before entering a trade; the set-up, trigger and confirmation. The confirmation provides evidence that the trigger has been breached.

Consolidation

Also known as range trading, prices simply move between two defined points. Price actually spends most of its time consolidating.

Crash

That thing most traders spend their lives worrying about. Crashes are extremely rare despite the modern folklore. In the past 50 years there have been two major crashes in Western markets; the broad market collapse in 1987 and the collapse of the Nasdaq in 2000.

Markets do enter bearish phases, such as 1974, where prices slowly move lower and lower, but very rarely do bear markets begin with a cataclysmic move down.

Day only order

An order that remains open until the close of the trading day.

Day trading

The buying and selling of instruments within a given trading day. Profitable if you can do it, the problem is only a very, very few traders can do it. Day trading is also the source of much mythology in that it is thought by people who are new to markets that day traders make all the money. The evidence would suggest this is a myth and that the majority of day traders (in excess of 90%) lose money.

Default

A bad thing; it is a failure to honour your obligation to the exchange where you are trading. Traders who default should be shot.

Deposit

Traders in derivatives markets have to lodge a deposit or initial margin with the exchange where a contingent liability exists (all futures contracts and naked written options positions).

Directional Movement Index

Directional movement uses a rather complicated set of calculations designed to rate the directional movement of commodities or stocks on a scale from 0 to 100. For those traders who employ trend-following methods, commodities or stocks rating in the upper end of the scale would be attractive. For those using non-trending methods, commodities or stocks rating at the lower end of the scale should be considered for trading. At its most basic, the directional movement would affect trading in the following manner: Long positions would be taken when the '+DI' line crosses over the '-DI' line. Short positions would be taken when the '-DI' line crosses over the '+DI' line.

Discount

An options trading term. An option is said to be trading at a discount when it is trading at less than its intrinsic value.

Discretionary account

A process whereby someone else such as a broker manages your money for you. A very bad idea. If brokers could make someone rich through being able to trade then who is the first person they would make rich?

Downside protection

Insurance against a downside move often achieved by the purchase of put options or warrants or the sale of an appropriate futures contract.

Downtrend

A period during which price makes lower and lower highs.

Early exercise

A nasty experience if you are an options trader, it refers to a given contract being exercised before its expiry date.

Endowment warrant

A warrant whereby the outstanding balance is paid for by the accumulation of dividends from the underlying share.

European option

An option that may only be exercised on the day of expiry.

Exchange-traded option

An option to take up an underlying security.

Exhaustion gap

This is a gap that occurs on the terminal phase of a move. It is a last ditch effort by either bulls or bears to push prices in the same way. It is an early warning signal that the move is faltering.

Exercise

To invoke the right granted under the terms of an options contract. For example if I own a call option I have the right to buy the underlying security.

Herrick Payoff Index

This is a commodity trading tool for the early spotting of changes in price trend direction. The Payoff Index is best used to distinguish trends that are destined to continue from those that will most likely be short-lived.

Historical volatility

A measure of how far price has moved over a given time.

In the money

When the exercise price of a call (put) is below (above) the current market value of the underlying security.

Intrinsic value

In the money options are said to possess intrinsic value. This is defined as the difference between the exercise price of the option and the price of the underlying contract.

Kagi Chart

Kagi charts display a series of connecting vertical lines where the thickness and direction of the lines are dependent on the price action. If closing prices continue to move in the direction of the prior vertical Kagi line, then that line is extended. However, if the closing price reverses by a predetermined 'reversal' amount, a new Kagi line is drawn in the next column in the opposite direction. An interesting aspect of the Kagi chart is that when closing prices penetrate the prior column's high or low, the thickness of the Kagi line changes.

Legging it in

A mechanism whereby trades that involve many variables such as complex spreads are done one leg at a time rather than simultaneously.

Liquid market

A prerequisite for successful trading; a liquid market is one with a great deal of turnover, which promotes rapid and clean price discovery.

MACD (Moving Average Convergence/Divergence)

The MACD is used to determine overbought or oversold conditions in the market. Written for stocks and stock indices, the MACD can be used for commodities as well. The MACD line is the difference between the long and short exponential moving averages of the chosen item. The signal line is an exponential moving average of the MACD line. Signals are generated by the relationship of the two lines. As with the RSI and Stochastic, divergences between the MACD and price may indicate an upcoming trend reversal.

Margin call

That dreaded phone call from either broker or margin lender saying we need more money. A succession of margin calls is generally an indication that you have got it wrong.

Market order

An order to buy or sell irrespective of the prevailing price.

Momentum

Momentum provides an analysis of changes in prices (as opposed to changes in price levels). Changes in the rate of ascent or descent are plotted. The momentum line is graphed positive or negative to a straight line representing time. The position of the timeline is determined by price at the beginning of the momentum period. Traders use this analysis to determine overbought and oversold conditions. When a maximum positive point is reached, the market is said to be overbought and a downward reaction is imminent. When a maximum negative point is reached, the market is said to be oversold and an upward reaction is indicated.

Money management

That very nebulous concept that most traders know nothing about. It covers concepts such as position sizing, pyramiding and stop loss points.

Moving averages

The moving average is probably the best-known and least understood indicator in the traders' arsenal. As the name implies, the moving average is the average of a given amount of data. For example, a 14-day average of closing prices is calculated by adding the last 14 closes and dividing by 14. Variations of the basic moving average are the weighted and exponential moving averages, or whatever is trendy this week. Useless in a congesting market

On Balance Volume (OBV)

Developed by Joseph Granville. The total volume for each day is assigned a positive or negative value depending on whether prices closed higher or lower that day. A higher close results in the volume for that day getting a positive value, while a lower close results in negative value. A running total is kept by adding or subtracting each day's volume based on the direction of the close. The direction of the OBV line is the thing to watch, not the actual volume numbers.

Out of the money

A call option with a strike price higher than the current market price or a put option with a strike price lower than the underlying security.

Overbought

A relative term used to describe the perception that prices have been pushed up to what is thought to be an unsustainable level.

Oversold

The opposite of overbought.

Parabolic Stop and Reverse (SAR)

This is a time/price system for the automatic setting of stops. The stop is both a function of price and of time. The system allows a few days for market reaction after a trade is initiated, after which stops begin to move in more rapid incremental daily amounts in the direction the trade was initiated.

Price patterns

Price patterns are formations which appear on commodity and stock charts which have shown to have a certain degree of predictive value. Some of the most common patterns include: Head & Shoulders (bearish), Inverse Head & Shoulders (bullish), Double Top (bearish), Double Bottom (bullish), Triangles, Flags and Pennants (can be bullish or bearish depending on the prevailing trend).

Put option

The right but not the obligation to sell an underlying instrument.

Pyramid

The technique of adding additional capital to an already profitable position. A skill very few master.

Rally

An upward movement in price.

Rate of change

Rate of change is used to monitor momentum by making direct comparisons between current and past prices on a continual basis. The results can be used to determine the strength of price trends. Note: This study is the same as the momentum except that momentum uses subtraction in its calculations while rate of change uses division. The resulting lines of these two studies operated over the same data will look exactly the same—only the scale values will differ.

Resistance

A price point at which there is an expectation sellers will enter the market and cap any upward move. This expectation is based upon previous attempts to move beyond this price.

Retracement

A pullback in prices. Something any one who entered the market in the past three years thought was extinct.

Relative Strength Index (RSI)

This indicator was developed by Welles Wilder Jr. Relative strength is often used to identify price tops and bottoms by keying on specific levels (usually '30' and '70') on the RSI chart which is scaled from 0 to 100. The study is also useful to detect the following:

1. Movement which might not be as readily apparent on the bar chart.

2. Failure swings above 70 or below 30 which can warn of coming reversals.

3. Support and resistance levels.

4. Divergence between the RSI and price, which is often a useful reversal indicator.

The Relative Strength Index requires a certain amount of lead-up time in order to operate successfully.

Renko chart

The Renko charting method probably got its name from 'renga', which is the Japanese word for bricks. Renko charts are similar to Three Line Break charts except that in a Renko chart, a line is drawn in the direction of the prior move only if a fixed amount (i.e. the box size) has been exceeded. The bricks are always equal in size. Example:

With a five unit Renko chart, a 20-point rally is displayed as four equally-sized, five-unit high Renko bricks.

Short selling

The strategy of selling an instrument that you do not already own in the belief that it can be bought back at a lower price.

Stochastic

The Stochastic Indicator is based on the observation that as prices increase, closing prices tend to accumulate ever closer to the highs for the period. Conversely, as prices decrease, closing prices tend to accumulate ever closer to the lows for the period. Trading decisions are made with respect to divergence between % of 'D' (one of the two lines generated by the study) and the item's price. For example, when a commodity or stock makes a high, reacts, and subsequently moves to a higher high while corresponding peaks on the % of 'D' line make a high and then a lower high, a bearish divergence is indicated. When a commodity or stock has established a new low, reacts, and moves to a lower low while the corresponding low points on the % of 'D' line make a low and then a higher low, a bullish divergence is indicated. Traders act upon this divergence when the other line generated by the study (K) crosses on the right-hand side of the peak of the % of 'D' line in the case of a top, or on the right-hand side of the low point of the % of 'D' line in the case of a bottom. Two variations of the Stochastic Indicator are in use: regular and slow. When the regular plot of the Stochastic is too choppy, the slow version can often clarify the results by reducing the sensitivity of the calculations.

Stop loss

A prerequisite for successful trading. It is a predetermined point at which a trade is deemed to have gone wrong and should be exited.

Support

A point at which buyers are expected to move into the market and place a floor under price.

Swing Index

The Swing Index (primarily for use with commodity trading) attempts to determine real market direction, and changes in direction, by making use of the most significant comparisons between the results (Open–High–Low–Close) of the current and previous day's trading.

Tick

The minimum allowable price move for a share option or commodity.

Trigger

A chart pattern or technical indicator that convinces the trader to enter a position.

Uptrend

Prices are making higher and higher highs.

Volume

The level of trading activity or turnover in a given instrument.

INDEX

THE art OF TRADING

CONSULTANCY SERVICES

Trading Seminars

Seminars are conducted regularly throughout the year in all capital cities and include the following topics:

➲ The Psychology of Trading

➲ Trading Method Design

➲ How to be a More Profitable Trader

➲ The Importance of the Trend.

For more information, contact:

info@artoftrading.com.au

PO Box 1171, North Caulfield, Victoria, 3161

Also by Christopher Tate...

THE ART OF
OPTIONS
TRADING
IN AUSTRALIA

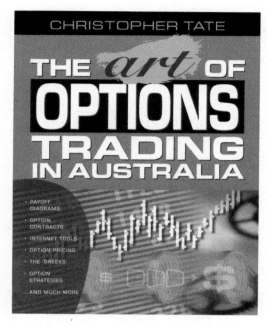

The exchange-traded options market is one of the most dynamic and innovative markets in Australia, and options themselves are amongst the most profitable tools available to traders. While traditional investors can only make a profit when the market is rising, traders in options can make money whether the market is moving up or down. The leverage they provide also allows traders to control a large amount of stock with a comparatively small amount of money.

In *The Art of Options Trading in Australia*, experienced and highly successful options trader Christopher Tate will show you how to make the most of these valuable tools. Starting with the basics of defining options, Chris goes on to look at:

- ➲ How options are priced, and what factors influence this
- ➲ Reading option quotes and payoff diagrams
- ➲ How the passing of time and changes in volatility affect options
- ➲ The 'Greeks' and how to use them
- ➲ Using the internet to assist your options trading
- ➲ Spreads, straddles and strangles
- ➲ Warrants, and the different types available.

Printed in Australia
20 Nov 2024
LP037418